Cloud Computing with AWS: Build and Deploy Apps in the Cloud

A Complete Guide to Understanding and Using AWS for Development

BOOZMAN RICHARD

BOOKER BLUNT

Table of Content

TABLE OF CONTENTS

INTRODUCTION

In the rapidly evolving world of cloud computing, mastering the tools and services offered by AWS (Amazon Web Services) has become a critical skill for professionals in the tech industry. **"Cloud Computing with AWS: Build and Deploy Apps in the Cloud"** is a comprehensive guide designed to equip you with the knowledge and skills needed to harness the power of AWS to build, deploy, and manage modern applications in the cloud.

Whether you are just starting your journey in cloud computing, or you're an experienced professional looking to expand your skill set, this book is designed to serve as both a foundational resource and a practical guide. It's ideal for anyone interested in gaining hands-on experience with AWS, whether you're preparing for an AWS certification exam, working on cloud-based applications for your company, or looking to develop a deeper understanding of AWS's vast service offerings.

What You Will Learn

This book covers all essential aspects of AWS cloud computing, from the basics to more advanced topics. You'll start by understanding the core concepts of cloud computing

6

and AWS itself, diving into the many services AWS offers, such as **EC2, S3, RDS, IAM**, and **Lambda**. You'll also learn how to build, deploy, and manage scalable applications, leveraging the full suite of AWS tools at your disposal.

Key topics explored in this book include:

- **Cloud Basics**: Learn the fundamentals of cloud computing and how AWS enables scalable, cost-efficient applications.
- **AWS Core Services**: Dive deep into essential AWS services such as **EC2, S3, IAM**, and **RDS**—the building blocks of AWS-based applications.
- **Microservices and Containers**: Learn how to deploy and manage microservices using **ECS** (Elastic Container Service) and **EKS** (Elastic Kubernetes Service).
- **Serverless Computing**: Discover the power of serverless architectures using **AWS Lambda** to reduce operational overhead and simplify application development.
- **DevOps and CI/CD**: Explore best practices for automating software development and deployment using **AWS CodePipeline** and other DevOps tools.

- **Security and Networking**: Master advanced networking concepts such as **VPC Peering** and **Transit Gateways**, and implement security best practices for AWS environments using **IAM** and encryption.

Through practical, real-world examples and case studies, you'll not only understand the theoretical concepts behind AWS services, but also learn how to implement them in real-world projects. From setting up basic services like storage and computing instances to deploying complex, multi-region, highly available architectures, this book guides you through every step of the way.

Who Should Read This Book?

This book is intended for a wide range of audiences, from beginners to intermediate-level professionals. It's perfect for:

- **Aspiring Cloud Professionals**: If you're just starting with cloud computing or AWS, this book provides a clear, easy-to-follow path to understanding the core AWS services and how to leverage them for real-world applications.

- **Developers**: If you're a software developer looking to learn how to deploy applications in the cloud, this book teaches you how to take advantage of AWS's compute, storage, and networking services to build robust, scalable applications.

- **System Administrators and DevOps Engineers**: Learn how to automate, monitor, and manage AWS-based infrastructure and applications with AWS's extensive suite of tools.

- **Students and Certification Candidates**: This book is an excellent resource if you're preparing for AWS certification exams, including the **Solutions Architect**, **Developer**, and **SysOps** certifications. The topics covered throughout the book align closely with AWS certification objectives, making it a comprehensive study guide.

- **Business Decision Makers**: If you're a business leader interested in understanding how AWS can drive innovation and cost savings in your organization, this book provides valuable insights into cloud adoption, security, and cost optimization strategies.

Why This Book is Different

Unlike traditional textbooks that are theoretical and abstract, **"Cloud Computing with AWS"** is built around **hands-on** learning. Each chapter is designed to provide you with actionable knowledge and practical examples that you can immediately apply to your own AWS environments. By the end of this book, you will not only have a strong grasp of AWS services but also the confidence to implement them effectively in real-world scenarios.

Additionally, the book's **step-by-step approach** ensures that you don't just learn concepts but also acquire practical skills. With **real-world case studies** and **advanced topics**, you will be well-prepared to tackle complex challenges in cloud architecture and application deployment.

The Path to Mastering AWS

This book is structured in a way that takes you from **beginner** to **advanced** topics. As you progress through the chapters, you'll gain a strong foundational knowledge of AWS, which will serve as the building block for more advanced topics such as microservices, serverless computing, and **DevOps** automation. The **hands-on**

examples and **real-world case studies** will reinforce your understanding and prepare you for actual deployment scenarios.

You'll begin with the basics—understanding what AWS is, how it works, and the services it provides. Then, as you build your knowledge and confidence, you'll move into more complex areas, such as:

- Building **scalable web applications** using AWS services like **EC2**, **S3**, and **RDS**.
- Designing and deploying **microservices** using **ECS** and **EKS**.
- Automating deployments with **CI/CD pipelines** using **AWS CodePipeline** and **CodeBuild**.
- Leveraging AWS's advanced networking features and security best practices to protect and optimize your applications.

By the time you finish this book, you will not only be able to manage AWS resources with confidence, but also be ready to design, build, and deploy sophisticated cloud-based applications that can scale, perform, and secure your workloads on AWS.

Get Ready for the Future of Cloud Computing

The world of cloud computing is evolving rapidly, and AWS continues to be a leader in providing innovative and scalable cloud services. This book will ensure that you are at the forefront of cloud technology, prepared to build the next generation of applications in a fast-paced, constantly changing cloud environment.

By the end of this book, you will have gained the practical knowledge to confidently design, build, and manage cloud applications in AWS. You will be empowered to navigate complex cloud architectures and deliver applications that are not only scalable and reliable but also secure and cost-efficient. Whether you are just getting started or looking to enhance your AWS expertise, this book will serve as your go-to guide for mastering **AWS cloud services** and **cloud computing architecture**.

CHAPTER 1

INTRODUCTION TO CLOUD COMPUTING AND AWS

Overview of Cloud Computing

Cloud computing refers to the delivery of computing services—such as servers, storage, databases, networking, software, and analytics—over the internet, or "the cloud." This allows businesses to avoid maintaining physical servers or data centers, reducing capital costs while increasing efficiency.

What is Cloud Computing? At its core, cloud computing allows individuals and organizations to access computing resources over the internet rather than relying on local servers or personal devices. The cloud provides scalability, reliability, and efficiency for a variety of applications, from hosting websites to running complex machine learning models.

Types of Cloud Services Cloud computing offers three primary types of services, each catering to different needs:

1. **Infrastructure as a Service (IaaS):**
   o Provides virtualized computing resources like virtual machines, storage, and networking over the internet.

13

- o **Example**: Amazon Web Services (AWS), Microsoft Azure, Google Cloud.
- o **Use Case**: A company needs scalable compute resources for running web applications or data storage without maintaining their own hardware.

2. **Platform as a Service (PaaS)**:
   - o Provides a platform that allows developers to build, run, and manage applications without worrying about the underlying infrastructure.
   - o **Example**: AWS Elastic Beanstalk, Google App Engine, Microsoft Azure App Service.
   - o **Use Case**: A developer builds and deploys a web application without worrying about server management.

3. **Software as a Service (SaaS)**:
   - o Delivers software applications over the internet on a subscription basis, eliminating the need for installation, maintenance, and management on local devices.
   - o **Example**: Google Workspace (formerly G Suite), Dropbox, Salesforce.
   - o **Use Case**: An organization uses a cloud-based customer relationship management (CRM) tool without maintaining any infrastructure.

Cloud Deployment Models Cloud deployment models define how cloud resources are made available and who controls them:

1. **Public Cloud**:
   - o Services are delivered over the internet and are available to anyone who wants to purchase or rent them.
   - o **Example**: AWS, Microsoft Azure, Google Cloud.
   - o **Use Case**: A business using AWS EC2 instances for scalable computing power.

2. **Private Cloud**:
   - o The infrastructure is dedicated to a single organization and is not shared with others, providing greater control over security and privacy.
   - o **Example**: A company's internal cloud for running its private applications.
   - o **Use Case**: A financial institution needs to maintain strict control over its data.

3. **Hybrid Cloud**:
   - o Combines both private and public clouds, allowing for data and applications to be shared between them.
   - o **Example**: A business that uses AWS for public services while maintaining an internal private cloud for sensitive applications.

o   **Use Case**: A healthcare organization uses a private cloud for patient data but leverages the public cloud for web hosting.

AWS Overview

What AWS Offers Amazon Web Services (AWS) is one of the leading cloud platforms in the world, offering a comprehensive suite of cloud computing services. These services include computing power (EC2), storage solutions (S3), database management (RDS, DynamoDB), networking, machine learning, IoT, and more. AWS caters to businesses of all sizes, from startups to large enterprises, and supports a wide range of use cases.

How AWS Works AWS operates on a pay-as-you-go model, where customers pay only for the resources they use. Customers can provision and scale resources through the AWS Management Console, command-line interface (CLI), or programmatically using AWS SDKs. AWS's global infrastructure is built on a network of data centers called Availability Zones (AZs) in multiple regions worldwide, ensuring high availability, reliability, and low latency.

Global Infrastructure AWS operates in multiple regions across the globe, each region containing multiple availability zones. These data centers are designed for high security and low latency,

16

and customers can choose where to host their services to meet local data sovereignty requirements.

AWS Pricing Model AWS follows a pay-as-you-go pricing model, where businesses only pay for what they use. This includes pricing for services like compute power, storage, and data transfer. Additionally, AWS provides options like Reserved Instances for cost savings on long-term use and Spot Instances for more affordable compute resources during off-peak times. AWS also offers cost management tools such as the AWS Cost Explorer and AWS Budgets.

Benefits of Cloud Computing

1. **Cost Efficiency**:
   - Traditional on-premises infrastructure requires significant upfront capital investment in hardware and maintenance. With cloud computing, businesses can avoid these large capital expenditures and switch to a more predictable operational cost model based on usage.
   - **Example**: A startup doesn't need to purchase expensive servers and can instead pay for cloud services only when they are needed.
2. **Scalability**:

17

- o Cloud computing offers the ability to quickly scale up or down depending on demand, providing flexibility in resource management. This is particularly useful for businesses with fluctuating needs.
- o **Example**: An eCommerce website can automatically scale its cloud resources during the holiday shopping season to accommodate increased traffic.

3. **Flexibility**:

- o The cloud allows for a wide variety of services, from web hosting to machine learning, which can be easily integrated and customized to meet business needs.
- o **Example**: A business can integrate cloud-based machine learning models with its existing applications to automate customer service or product recommendations.

4. **Security**:

- o AWS and other cloud providers offer advanced security features, such as encryption, firewalls, and dedicated security teams, making it easier for businesses to implement strong security measures.

o **Example**: A financial institution can ensure its sensitive customer data is encrypted and accessible only by authorized personnel.

Real-World Example: A Startup Migrating from On-Premises Infrastructure to AWS

Let's consider a startup that has been operating with traditional on-premises servers for hosting its application. Over time, as the business grows, the need for scaling resources (CPU, memory, storage) becomes more apparent. The startup's IT team faces challenges in maintaining hardware, managing server capacity, and ensuring uptime.

By migrating to AWS, the startup can immediately take advantage of EC2 instances for compute power, S3 for storage, and RDS for database management without having to purchase and manage physical hardware. AWS's pay-as-you-go model means the startup only pays for the resources it uses, allowing for efficient cost management and eliminating the need for upfront capital expenditures. Additionally, with AWS's scalability, the startup can easily adjust its infrastructure based on usage, enabling them to meet growing demands and reduce over-provisioning costs.

As the startup continues to grow, AWS provides a solid foundation for handling increased website traffic, processing more transactions, and adding new services—all while maintaining high availability and security.

This chapter provides an essential introduction to the core concepts of cloud computing and how AWS empowers businesses to leverage the cloud for development, storage, and deployment. In the following chapters, we will dive deeper into specific AWS services and how to use them to build and deploy applications effectively.

CHAPTER 2

SETTING UP AN AWS ACCOUNT AND BASIC NAVIGATION

Creating and Configuring an AWS Account: Step-by-Step Setup

To begin using AWS, you'll need to create an AWS account. Follow these simple steps to get started:

1. **Sign Up for an AWS Account**
   - Visit AWS's sign-up page, and click on **Create an AWS Account**.
   - Enter your email address, choose a password, and enter your account name. This will be your AWS root account, so ensure it is a secure email and password combination.
   - **Tip**: Use an email that is dedicated to managing your AWS account for security reasons.

2. **Enter Payment Information**
   - AWS offers a **free tier**, but you will still need to enter a credit or debit card for verification purposes. You won't be charged for free-tier services, but charges will apply if you exceed the free-tier limits.

3. **Verify Your Identity**

o   AWS may require you to verify your identity via phone number. You'll receive an automated call and need to enter a PIN to confirm your identity.

4. **Choose a Support Plan**

o   AWS offers different support plans, ranging from basic (free) to enterprise-level support. For now, choose the **Basic Support Plan** to get started without additional costs.

5. **Complete the Setup**

o   After verification, you'll be directed to the AWS Management Console, where you can start configuring services and managing your AWS resources.

Once your account is set up, it's time to familiarize yourself with the AWS Management Console and its tools.

AWS Management Console: Navigation, Creating Your First EC2 Instance, Setting Up IAM Roles

The **AWS Management Console** is the web-based interface used to manage AWS services. Let's break down some basic tasks you'll need to perform in the console:

1. **Navigating the AWS Management Console**

- o After logging into your AWS account, the first page you will see is the **AWS Management Console Dashboard**. Here, you can quickly access all AWS services via the search bar or by navigating through categories like **Compute**, **Storage**, **Databases**, etc.
- o **Tip**: You can customize your console's layout for quicker access to frequently used services.

2. **Creating Your First EC2 Instance** Amazon EC2 (Elastic Compute Cloud) is one of the core services that allows you to run virtual machines in the cloud. To create your first EC2 instance:

- o **Step 1**: Navigate to **EC2** under the "Compute" section.
- o **Step 2**: Click **Launch Instance**.
- o **Step 3**: Select an **Amazon Machine Image (AMI)**. For a simple start, choose the **Amazon Linux 2 AMI** (free tier eligible).
- o **Step 4**: Select an **Instance Type**. Start with the **t2.micro** instance, which is eligible for the free tier.
- o **Step 5**: Configure your instance. Set the number of instances, network settings, and other configurations (you can accept default settings for now).

- o **Step 6**: Add **Storage**. The default 8 GB storage is sufficient for a simple test instance.
- o **Step 7**: Add **Tags**. This step is optional but useful for organization. Tag your instance with a name like "MyFirstEC2".
- o **Step 8**: Configure **Security Groups**. Select "Create a new security group" to set up basic firewall rules for your instance. For now, allow **SSH** access on port 22 to connect remotely.
- o **Step 9**: Review the configuration, then click **Launch**.
- o **Step 10**: **Select a key pair**. If you don't have one already, create a new one and download the private key file (this is important for SSH access).

After the instance is launched, you can connect to it via SSH using the key pair you downloaded. Use the **Elastic IP** assigned to your instance to access it remotely.

3. **Setting Up IAM Roles** AWS IAM (Identity and Access Management) is crucial for securely managing who can access your AWS resources. Here's how to set up basic IAM roles:

- o **Step 1**: Navigate to the **IAM** service in the AWS Console.
- o **Step 2**: Click on **Roles** in the left-hand menu and then **Create Role**.

24

- o **Step 3**: Choose a role type. For now, select **EC2** to grant the instance permissions to access other AWS resources.
- o **Step 4**: Attach policies. For a basic setup, choose the **AmazonEC2FullAccess** policy to give your EC2 instance full access to EC2 resources.
- o **Step 5**: Name the role, such as "MyEC2Role" and finish the setup.

After this, you can assign this IAM role to your EC2 instances when launching them, providing them with the necessary permissions.

Real-World Example: A Small Business Setting Up AWS to Host Their Website

Imagine a small business that has traditionally hosted its website on local servers. The business is growing and experiencing increasing web traffic, so they decide to migrate to the cloud for greater scalability and reliability. Here's how they can use AWS to host their website:

1. **Setting Up an EC2 Instance** The business begins by creating an EC2 instance to host their website. Using the steps above, they create a **t2.micro EC2 instance** running Amazon Linux 2 AMI. This provides a lightweight, cost-

effective solution for hosting a basic website. They also install a web server (like **Apache** or **Nginx**) on the EC2 instance to serve their website content.

2. **Configuring Security Groups** The business configures a security group to allow HTTP (port 80) and HTTPS (port 443) access to their web server. They also ensure that only authorized users can access the instance via SSH by setting up proper key pair authentication.

3. **Setting Up S3 for Media Storage** To avoid overloading the EC2 instance with large media files (e.g., images or videos), the business uses **Amazon S3** for scalable storage. They create an S3 bucket and upload media files to it, linking the files to their website for faster loading times.

4. **Managing Access with IAM Roles** The business's development team creates IAM roles for the website's resources. For example, they assign a role to the EC2 instance that allows it to interact with S3 to retrieve and serve media files.

5. **Scaling with Auto Scaling and Load Balancing** As the business grows, they use **Auto Scaling** to automatically adjust the number of EC2 instances based on web traffic. They also set up an **Elastic Load Balancer (ELB)** to distribute incoming traffic evenly across multiple EC2 instances, ensuring high availability and reliability.

6. **Using Route 53 for DNS Management** The business uses **Amazon Route 53** for domain name system (DNS) management. They register their domain and configure Route 53 to route users to their website hosted on AWS.

By setting up AWS for their website hosting, the business benefits from cost-effective, scalable infrastructure, ensuring smooth performance as the business grows. With the ability to scale up or down based on traffic, they no longer worry about over-provisioning or downtime due to traffic spikes.

In this chapter, we've learned how to create and configure an AWS account, navigate the AWS Management Console, set up EC2 instances, configure security settings with IAM roles, and deploy a simple website. As we move into the next chapters, we'll explore more advanced features and services AWS offers for developing and deploying complex applications.

CHAPTER 3

AWS CORE SERVICES OVERVIEW

In this chapter, we will dive into the core AWS services that form the foundation of cloud applications: **EC2**, **S3**, **RDS**, and **IAM**. These services are essential for building scalable, reliable, and secure applications in the cloud. Understanding how each of these services works and how to use them together will enable you to build robust cloud solutions.

EC2 (Elastic Compute Cloud): Virtual Servers in the Cloud

Amazon EC2 provides scalable virtual servers in the cloud. With EC2, you can run applications on a virtual machine (VM), providing the computing power you need while allowing you to scale your infrastructure based on demand.

Choosing EC2 Instance Types When setting up an EC2 instance, you'll choose from a variety of instance types, each designed for specific use cases. EC2 instances are categorized into families based on their resources (CPU, memory, storage), and the choice of instance depends on your application's requirements.

28

- **General Purpose**: Instances like **t2.micro** are suited for low-traffic websites or small applications.
- **Compute Optimized**: Instances like **c5** are ideal for applications requiring high computational power, such as scientific computing or high-performance web servers.
- **Memory Optimized**: Instances like **r5** are optimized for workloads that require large amounts of memory, such as in-memory caches or high-performance databases.
- **Storage Optimized**: Instances like **i3** are designed for applications requiring high I/O performance and storage, like big data analytics.
- **Accelerated Computing**: Instances like **p3** are optimized for machine learning and GPU-based applications.

Setting Up EC2

- To launch an EC2 instance, navigate to the **EC2 Dashboard** in the AWS Console, choose an AMI (Amazon Machine Image), select an instance type based on your workload, configure the instance, and set up security groups to control access.
- After launching, you can SSH into the instance (for Linux) or use Remote Desktop Protocol (RDP) for Windows to begin setting up your application.

Real-World Example: Deploying a simple web server on an EC2 instance that serves a static website.

S3 (Simple Storage Service): Object Storage, Creating and Managing Buckets

Amazon S3 is an object storage service that allows you to store and retrieve any amount of data. It's widely used for storing static files like images, videos, backups, and log files. The key feature of S3 is that it offers virtually unlimited storage, making it highly scalable for your data needs.

Creating and Managing Buckets

- **Buckets**: A bucket is a container for storing objects. Each S3 object consists of data (such as a file), metadata, and a unique identifier (key).
- **Naming Buckets**: Buckets must have globally unique names. For example, "my-website-images".
- **Uploading Objects**: You can upload files to an S3 bucket via the AWS Management Console, AWS CLI, or programmatically using AWS SDKs.

Managing Permissions and Security

- **Bucket Policies**: You can define who can access your S3 bucket and what actions they can perform. For example, you can allow public access to an image bucket while keeping a private backup bucket secure.

30

- **Versioning**: S3 allows you to keep multiple versions of an object. This feature is useful for managing backups or tracking changes to documents over time.
- **Lifecycle Policies**: You can set lifecycle policies to automatically transition objects between storage classes (e.g., moving files from S3 Standard to S3 Glacier for archival purposes) or delete them after a certain period.

Real-World Example: Using S3 to store images and videos for a media-sharing app. These assets are uploaded to S3 and linked to the website for fast access.

RDS (Relational Database Service): Setting Up Databases in the Cloud

Amazon RDS is a managed relational database service that allows you to easily set up, operate, and scale databases in the cloud. It supports several database engines, including **MySQL**, **PostgreSQL**, **MariaDB**, **Oracle**, and **SQL Server**.

Setting Up an RDS Instance

- **Choosing a Database Engine**: AWS offers several RDS engines. MySQL is popular for open-source applications, while SQL Server is typically used for enterprise-level applications.

- **Database Instance Types**: Just like EC2, you will choose an instance type for your database based on performance needs. You can select instances with varying amounts of CPU, memory, and storage.
- **Multi-AZ and Read Replicas**: AWS RDS offers high availability through **Multi-AZ deployments**. This ensures that your database is replicated across multiple availability zones for fault tolerance. Additionally, **Read Replicas** allow for scaling read-heavy workloads by creating copies of the database for read-only queries.
- **Automatic Backups**: RDS automatically backs up your databases daily, enabling you to restore to any point within the retention period.

Connecting to RDS

- Once your RDS instance is created, you can connect to it using the database endpoint provided in the AWS Console. From there, you can use SQL clients or programmatically connect via your application.

Real-World Example: Hosting the user database for a social media platform in an RDS MySQL instance to handle user authentication, profiles, and posts.

IAM (Identity and Access Management): Secure User Management and Access Control

AWS IAM is a powerful service that enables you to securely control access to AWS services and resources. By managing users, groups, and permissions, IAM helps ensure that only authorized individuals or services can access sensitive resources.

Creating IAM Users and Groups

- **Users**: An IAM user is an entity that you create to represent a person or application that needs access to your AWS resources. Each user is assigned a unique set of credentials.
- **Groups**: IAM groups are collections of IAM users. You can assign permissions to the group, and all members inherit those permissions.
- **Permissions**: AWS uses **policies** to define permissions. Policies are attached to users or groups and specify what actions can be performed on which AWS resources.

Roles and Temporary Security Credentials

- **IAM Roles**: A role is an AWS identity with specific permissions that can be assumed by trusted entities, such as EC2 instances, Lambda functions, or IAM users. Roles are useful for delegating permissions without sharing long-term credentials.

- **Temporary Security Credentials**: These credentials are used by applications or services to access AWS resources for a limited period. They are ideal for temporary access needs and can be automatically rotated.

Best Practices for IAM

- **Least Privilege Principle**: Grant users the least amount of access necessary to perform their tasks. This minimizes potential security risks.
- **Enable MFA**: Enabling Multi-Factor Authentication (MFA) for IAM users adds an extra layer of security.

Real-World Example: An administrator creating IAM roles for a development team. The admin grants the developers permissions to launch EC2 instances and access S3 buckets while limiting permissions on other services like RDS.

Real-World Example: Deploying a Basic App with an EC2 Instance, S3 Storage, and RDS for Data Storage

Let's walk through the steps of deploying a basic web application using EC2, S3, and RDS.

1. **EC2 Instance Setup**:
   o The business launches an EC2 instance using the **Amazon Linux 2** AMI.

- They install a web server (e.g., **Apache** or **Nginx**) on the instance to host their application.
- The instance is configured to serve static content (HTML, CSS, JavaScript) and dynamic content via PHP or another backend language.

2. **S3 Storage**:
   - The business uses **S3** to store user-uploaded files, such as images or documents. S3 allows fast and secure storage with global access.
   - The EC2 instance is configured to upload and retrieve files from S3 using AWS SDKs or the command line.

3. **RDS for Database**:
   - The web application uses **RDS** (MySQL) to manage user data. The RDS instance is configured for high availability with Multi-AZ deployment to ensure uptime.
   - The application connects to the database securely using the RDS endpoint.

4. **Security with IAM**:
   - IAM roles are created to give the EC2 instance access to S3 and RDS. These roles ensure that only authorized actions are performed on the resources.

o   The business follows best practices by granting IAM users only the permissions needed to deploy and manage the app.

By using these core AWS services, the business can easily manage and scale its application in the cloud. They get the benefits of high availability, security, and scalability, which are essential for growth.

In this chapter, we've explored the core AWS services—EC2, S3, RDS, and IAM—each playing a crucial role in building cloud-based applications. In the following chapters, we will dive deeper into advanced features, optimization strategies, and other services AWS has to offer for building robust cloud solutions.

CHAPTER 4

EC2 - LAUNCHING AND MANAGING VIRTUAL SERVERS

In this chapter, we'll explore **Amazon EC2 (Elastic Compute Cloud)**, which provides scalable virtual servers in the cloud. EC2 is one of the most fundamental and flexible services within AWS, and it allows businesses to run applications on virtual machines in the cloud, scaling resources based on demand. We will walk through the different types of EC2 instances, how to create and manage them, and how to securely access them using SSH.

Introduction to EC2 Instances: Types, Configurations, and Pricing

What is an EC2 Instance? An **EC2 instance** is a virtual server that runs in the AWS cloud. You can launch, configure, and manage EC2 instances to run various applications, such as web servers, databases, or custom business applications. Each instance has its own operating system, disk storage, and networking configuration.

Types of EC2 Instances EC2 instances are categorized into different types based on their intended use. Each type offers a specific balance of CPU, memory, storage, and networking performance. Below are the primary categories:

1. **General Purpose**:
   o These instances provide a balance of compute, memory, and networking resources. Suitable for most common workloads like web servers or development environments.
   o **Example: t3.micro, t2.micro** (eligible for the AWS Free Tier).

2. **Compute Optimized**:
   o Designed for compute-intensive applications, such as high-performance web servers, batch processing, and scientific modeling.
   o **Example: c5.large, c4.xlarge**.

3. **Memory Optimized**:
   o These instances are ideal for workloads that require a large amount of memory, such as in-memory databases or real-time big data processing.
   o **Example: r5.large, x1e.16xlarge**.

4. **Storage Optimized**:
   o These instances provide high throughput and low-latency disk I/O for workloads requiring intensive storage, such as NoSQL databases and large-scale data processing.
   o **Example: i3.large, d2.8xlarge**.

5. **Accelerated Computing**:

   o Instances equipped with GPU or FPGA (Field Programmable Gate Array) hardware for specialized workloads such as machine learning, video encoding, or scientific simulations.

   o **Example**: **p3.2xlarge, inf1.xlarge**.

Pricing of EC2 Instances EC2 pricing depends on the instance type, the region where the instance is hosted, and the specific configurations (e.g., storage, number of instances). AWS offers different pricing models:

1. **On-Demand Instances**: Pay per hour or second based on the instance type, with no long-term commitment.

2. **Reserved Instances**: Commit to using an instance for a one- or three-year term in exchange for a significant discount.

3. **Spot Instances**: Bid for unused capacity and take advantage of cheaper prices, though these instances can be terminated with short notice by AWS.

Free Tier: For those just getting started, AWS provides a **Free Tier**, which includes 750 hours per month of **t2.micro** or **t3.micro** instances for the first 12 months.

To launch an EC2 instance, follow these steps:

1. **Log in to the AWS Management Console**
   - Navigate to **EC2** under the "Compute" section.

2. **Launch an Instance**
   - Click on the **Launch Instance** button to start the wizard for creating a new EC2 instance.

3. **Choose an Amazon Machine Image (AMI)**
   - An **AMI** is a pre-configured template for your EC2 instance, including an operating system, application server, and applications. You can choose from several pre-built AMIs, such as:
     - **Amazon Linux 2**
     - **Ubuntu**
     - **Windows Server**
   - For most use cases, **Amazon Linux 2** is a great choice, as it's optimized for EC2.

4. **Choose an Instance Type**
   - Select the instance type based on your workload. For example:
     - **t2.micro** for lightweight applications (Free Tier eligible).
     - **m5.large** for a balanced setup that can handle moderate traffic.

- **c5.large** for compute-intensive applications.
  - o AWS gives you a recommendation based on your usage patterns, or you can manually choose the right instance type.

5. **Configure Instance Details**
   - o Specify the number of instances you want to launch (e.g., 1).
   - o Configure **network settings** (e.g., VPC, subnet) and **IAM roles** (if necessary).
   - o You can leave most settings as default for basic usage, or customize them for high availability and scaling.

6. **Add Storage**
   - o You can add **EBS (Elastic Block Store)** volumes to your instance for additional storage. By default, EC2 comes with an 8 GB **EBS** volume, but you can modify it based on your needs.
   - o AWS allows you to choose from different **EBS types**, such as General Purpose SSD or Provisioned IOPS SSD, depending on your performance requirements.

7. **Configure Security Group**
   - o A **security group** acts as a firewall that controls inbound and outbound traffic to your instance. For a basic web server:

41

- Open ports **80 (HTTP)** and **443 (HTTPS)** to allow web traffic.
- Open **22 (SSH)** for Linux instances or **3389 (RDP)** for Windows instances to allow remote access.
  - You can configure additional rules based on your requirements.

8. **Review and Launch**
   - Review your configurations, then click **Launch**.
   - When prompted, create a new **key pair** for SSH access (for Linux instances) or download your existing key pair. Store the private key file securely, as it is required to access your instance.

SSH Access to EC2: Accessing and Managing EC2 Servers Securely

Once your EC2 instance is running, you will need to access it remotely. For Linux-based EC2 instances, this is done via **SSH** (Secure Shell). Here's how to access your instance:

1. **Locate Your Private Key File**
   - When you launched the instance, you were prompted to create or select a **key pair**. Ensure you have the **.pem** file (private key) on your local machine.

2. **Change Permissions for the Key File**

o Ensure the private key file has the correct permissions:

```
bash
```

```
chmod 400 /path/to/your-key.pem
```

3. **Find Your EC2 Instance's Public IP**

   o From the **EC2 Dashboard**, select your instance, and find the **Public IP** or **Elastic IP** associated with the instance.

4. **SSH into the EC2 Instance**

   o Open your terminal and connect to the instance:

```
bash
```

```
ssh   -i   /path/to/your-key.pem   ec2-
user@your-ec2-public-ip
```

   o Replace /path/to/your-key.pem with the actual path to your private key file, and your-ec2-public-ip with the public IP of your EC2 instance.

5. **Managing EC2 Instance via SSH**

   o Once connected, you can install and manage your software, configure your server, and perform any other tasks you need.

Real-World Example: Hosting a Small Business Website on EC2 with a Static IP

Let's consider a small business that wants to host a simple website on AWS. The steps involved would be as follows:

1. **Create EC2 Instance**:
   - The business launches a **t2.micro** EC2 instance with **Amazon Linux 2 AMI** for the website.
   - They select the **t2.micro** instance type (eligible for the AWS Free Tier), which is enough for a low-traffic website.
2. **Install Web Server**:
   - After SSHing into the instance, the business installs a web server (Apache or Nginx) to serve the website:

bash

```
sudo yum install httpd -y  # For Apache on
Amazon Linux 2
sudo service httpd start
```

3. **Configure Static IP**:
   - The business associates an **Elastic IP** with their EC2 instance to ensure a fixed public IP address

that doesn't change after the instance is stopped or restarted.

4. **Deploy Website Files**:
   o The business uploads its website's HTML, CSS, and JavaScript files to the EC2 instance, and stores any user-uploaded files on **S3** for efficient file management.

5. **Set Up Security**:
   o The security group is configured to allow HTTP (port 80) and SSH (port 22) traffic. The website is now accessible at the static IP address.

6. **Launch and Monitor**:
   o After deploying the website, the business can monitor the EC2 instance's health using **CloudWatch** and scale the instance or add more resources if traffic increases.

By using EC2, the business is able to host its website in the cloud with minimal upfront costs and the ability to scale as needed.

In this chapter, we've covered the basics of EC2 instances, from selecting the right instance type and launching an instance to securely accessing it via SSH. We also explored how a small business can use EC2 to host a simple website. As we move forward, we will explore how to scale and optimize EC2 instances for more complex applications.

CHAPTER 5

S3 - SCALABLE OBJECT STORAGE

Amazon S3 (Simple Storage Service) is one of AWS's core services, designed to provide scalable object storage for a wide range of use cases, from web hosting to backup and disaster recovery. In this chapter, we will explore how to use S3 to store and manage data, configure lifecycle policies to optimize costs, and implement versioning and data retrieval strategies. We'll also look at a real-world example of how S3 can be used in a photo-sharing app to manage user-generated media files.

Using S3 for Storage: Uploading Files, Creating Buckets, Setting Permissions

What is S3 Storage? Amazon S3 is an object storage service that allows you to store and retrieve any amount of data from anywhere on the web. It's designed to be highly scalable, secure, and durable, making it an ideal solution for storing everything from website assets to backups and data archives.

Creating Buckets

- In S3, **buckets** are containers for storing objects (files). Each object is uniquely identified by a key, which is the object's name within the bucket. When you upload a file to S3, you are storing it in a bucket.

Steps to create a bucket:

1. Go to the **S3 Dashboard** in the AWS Management Console.
2. Click **Create Bucket**.
3. Enter a **unique bucket name** (bucket names must be globally unique).
4. Select a region where the bucket will be stored (typically, choose the region closest to your user base for faster access).
5. Set up **bucket permissions** (public or private) and review the settings.
6. Click **Create**.

Uploading Files to S3 Once your bucket is created, you can upload files to it via the AWS Management Console, AWS CLI, or programmatically using AWS SDKs.

1. **Console Method**: Navigate to your bucket and click the **Upload** button. You can select files to upload directly from your local machine or drag and drop them.

2. **CLI Method**: Use the AWS Command Line Interface (CLI) to upload files:

```bash
aws s3 cp /local/file.txt s3://your-bucket-name/
```

3. **SDK Method**: Use SDKs for popular programming languages like Python, Java, or Node.js to integrate S3 file uploads directly into your applications.

Setting Permissions and Security S3 provides fine-grained control over permissions, allowing you to specify who can access your buckets and objects. Permissions can be managed at both the bucket and object level.

- **Bucket Policies**: You can define a policy to control access to all objects in a bucket. For example, you can allow public access to a static website's assets or restrict access to a certain IAM role.
- **Access Control Lists (ACLs)**: ACLs allow you to define permissions for individual objects.
- **IAM Policies**: You can also use IAM roles and policies to manage access permissions to S3 buckets programmatically.

49

For instance, to make a bucket publicly accessible for serving website assets, you can add the following bucket policy:

json

```json
{
    "Version": "2012-10-17",
    "Statement": [
      {
        "Effect": "Allow",
        "Principal": "*",
        "Action": "s3:GetObject",
        "Resource":     "arn:aws:s3:::your-bucket-name/*"
      }
    ]
}
```

Lifecycle Policies: How to Set Up Storage Policies for Cost Management

AWS S3 Lifecycle Policies help automate the process of moving data to lower-cost storage classes or deleting data after a certain period. This is particularly useful for managing costs associated with storing large amounts of data.

Types of Storage Classes in S3:

1. **S3 Standard**: For frequently accessed data.
2. **S3 Intelligent-Tiering**: Automatically moves data to the most cost-effective storage tier based on access patterns.
3. **S3 Standard-IA (Infrequent Access)**: For data that is infrequently accessed but needs to be retrieved quickly when necessary.
4. **S3 One Zone-IA**: A lower-cost option for infrequently accessed data stored in a single availability zone.
5. **S3 Glacier**: For archival data that is rarely accessed, offering the lowest cost but slower retrieval times.
6. **S3 Glacier Deep Archive**: The lowest-cost storage for long-term archiving, with retrieval times ranging from hours to days.

Setting Up Lifecycle Policies To create a lifecycle policy:

1. Go to your **S3 bucket** in the AWS Management Console.
2. Click on the **Management** tab, then select **Lifecycle**.
3. Click **Create Lifecycle Rule**.
4. Define the rule's scope (either the entire bucket or specific folders).
5. Set actions for transitioning objects between storage classes:
   - o   Transition objects to **S3 Glacier** after 30 days.
   - o   Delete objects older than 365 days.

This helps reduce storage costs by moving less frequently accessed data to cheaper storage classes and deleting unnecessary data.

Versioning and Data Retrieval: Managing Versions and Retrieving Data

What is Versioning? S3 versioning enables you to keep multiple versions of an object in the same bucket. This is especially useful for managing and retrieving different versions of files, such as document revisions or media assets.

- **Enabling Versioning**: To enable versioning, navigate to the **Properties** tab of your S3 bucket and click **Enable versioning**. Once enabled, every time you upload a file with the same name, S3 will retain the previous version of that file.
- **Viewing Versions**: You can view and manage different versions of your objects by clicking on the file in the S3 Console and checking the version ID.

Retrieving Previous Versions

- To retrieve a previous version, select the object in your S3 bucket and click on **Version ID**. You can download an earlier version of the object or restore it as the current version.

Deleting Versions

- If you no longer need a version of an object, you can permanently delete it. By default, S3 will only delete the current version of an object, leaving older versions intact unless explicitly deleted.

Real-World Example: Using S3 to store user-generated media files for a photo-sharing app

Let's consider a photo-sharing app where users upload images, which are stored in S3. The app stores these media files in a dedicated S3 bucket, where each user's images are organized by user ID.

1. **Uploading User Images**:
   o Every time a user uploads a photo, the photo is stored in S3 with a unique object key (e.g., `userID/photoID.jpg`).
   o The app ensures that the user can access their media files quickly by uploading them to the **S3 Standard** storage class.
2. **Setting Up Lifecycle Policies**:
   o The app doesn't need to keep every user image forever. For example, photos older than one year

might no longer be accessed frequently. A lifecycle policy can be set to transition older photos to **S3 Glacier** or **S3 Glacier Deep Archive** for long-term storage at a lower cost.

o The policy could also automatically delete images that are older than three years, which reduces storage costs further.

3. **Managing Versions**:

o As users upload and update their photos, versioning is enabled for the bucket to ensure that older versions of an image are preserved in case of accidental deletion or modification.

o For example, if a user replaces an image, the old version is retained. The app can retrieve the previous version of the image if needed.

4. **Retrieving Data**:

o If a user requests to download their photo, the app retrieves the latest version from S3. If a user requests an older version (e.g., a previous photo), the app can query S3 by specifying the version ID.

By leveraging S3, the photo-sharing app can provide scalable storage for user-generated content, manage costs through lifecycle policies, and ensure data integrity with versioning. The app benefits from the high availability, durability, and security of S3, providing a reliable storage solution for its users.

In this chapter, we've covered how to use S3 for scalable object storage, how to set lifecycle policies to manage costs effectively, and how versioning and data retrieval work in S3. In the next chapters, we will dive deeper into advanced S3 features and how to integrate S3 with other AWS services to build more complex solutions.

CHAPTER 6

IAM - SECURING YOUR AWS RESOURCES

In this chapter, we'll explore **AWS Identity and Access Management (IAM)**, a critical service that allows you to securely manage users, groups, and permissions for AWS resources. IAM is essential for enforcing the principle of least privilege, ensuring that each individual or service has only the permissions they need to perform their tasks. By properly managing IAM, you can maintain security, compliance, and governance across your AWS environment.

Creating and Managing Users and Groups: Best Practices for User Management

What is IAM? AWS **IAM** is a service that allows you to manage access to AWS resources. You can create users, assign them to groups, and attach permissions to them. IAM also enables you to set policies and grant access to resources for both AWS services and users.

Creating IAM Users

- **IAM Users**: These are individual identities within your AWS account. Each user can have their own set of credentials (username and password or access keys) and be granted specific permissions.

- **Steps to Create a User**:

  1. Go to the **IAM Dashboard** in the AWS Management Console.

  2. Click on **Users** in the left-hand menu and click **Add user**.

  3. Enter the user's name and choose the type of access (e.g., **Programmatic access** for API access or **AWS Management Console access** for UI access).

  4. Set up permissions (attach existing policies or create custom ones).

  5. Review the user's configuration and click **Create User**.

  6. Make sure to save the **access credentials** securely. If the user is granted programmatic access, an **access key** will be generated.

Creating IAM Groups

- **IAM Groups**: Groups allow you to assign permissions to multiple users at once. Rather than assigning individual permissions to each user, you can create a group and assign permissions to the group. Any user added to the group will automatically inherit those permissions.

- **Steps to Create a Group**:
    1. In the **IAM Dashboard**, click on **Groups** and select **Create New Group**.
    2. Enter a name for the group (e.g., **Developers**, **Admins**, etc.).
    3. Attach appropriate permissions policies to the group (e.g., **AmazonEC2FullAccess**, **S3ReadOnlyAccess**).
    4. Add users to the group by selecting the users you want to include.

Best Practices for User Management

- **Principle of Least Privilege**: Only give users the permissions they need to perform their tasks. Avoid granting excessive permissions, especially with sensitive resources.
- **Avoid Using Root User**: The root user has unrestricted access to all resources. Use it only for account setup and administrative tasks. For daily operations, create IAM users with specific permissions.
- **Naming Conventions**: Use clear and descriptive names for IAM users and groups to help organize and manage your resources more efficiently.

Policies and Permissions: Defining Access Control Using IAM Policies

What are IAM Policies? IAM Policies define the permissions for an IAM user, group, or role. They are written in JSON (JavaScript Object Notation) format and specify who can do what with which AWS resources. Policies contain one or more statements, and each statement defines an action (e.g., `s3:ListBucket`, `ec2:StartInstances`), a resource (e.g., a specific S3 bucket or EC2 instance), and the effect (Allow or Deny).

Types of IAM Policies

1. **Managed Policies**:
   o AWS provides predefined, managed policies for common use cases, such as **AmazonEC2FullAccess** or **AmazonS3ReadOnlyAccess**.
   o These policies are easy to attach to users and groups.

2. **Inline Policies**:
   o These are policies that you create and attach directly to a user, group, or role. Inline policies are more specific and tightly coupled with the user or group.

59

3. **Custom Policies**:

   o You can write your own policies to meet specific access requirements. This provides full flexibility in defining permissions.

   o Example of a simple S3 read-only policy:

```
json
```

```json
{
  "Version": "2012-10-17",
  "Statement": [
    {
      "Effect": "Allow",
      "Action": "s3:GetObject",
      "Resource":     "arn:aws:s3:::your-
bucket-name/*"
    }
  ]
}
```

This policy allows a user to read objects in a specific S3 bucket.

Steps to Attach Policies:

1. After creating a user or group, navigate to the **Permissions** tab.

2. Click **Attach Policies** and select the relevant managed policies or custom policies.

3. Review and attach the policy.

Best Practices for Managing Permissions

- **Avoid Over-permissioning**: Do not assign broad permissions like `AdministratorAccess` unless absolutely necessary.

- **Use Groups to Manage Permissions**: Instead of assigning permissions to individual users, manage permissions via groups, making it easier to add or remove users with specific access needs.

- **Regularly Review and Audit Permissions**: Ensure that users only have the permissions they need, and remove any unnecessary permissions to minimize the attack surface.

Multi-Factor Authentication (MFA): Securing AWS Account Access

What is MFA? Multi-Factor Authentication (MFA) adds an extra layer of security to your AWS account. With MFA enabled, users must provide something they know (a password) and something they have (a code from a physical or virtual MFA device). This significantly reduces the risk of unauthorized access due to compromised credentials.

How to Enable MFA

1. Navigate to the **IAM Dashboard** and select **Users**.

2. Choose the user for which you want to enable MFA.

3. Under the **Security Credentials** tab, click **Manage MFA Device**.

4. Select the type of MFA device you are using (e.g., virtual MFA device like Google Authenticator or a hardware MFA device).

5. Follow the steps to associate the MFA device with the user account.

Best Practices for MFA

- **Enable MFA for All Users**: Particularly for accounts with access to sensitive data or resources, MFA should be mandatory.

- **Use Virtual MFA Devices**: Virtual MFA apps are easy to set up and cost-effective. Google Authenticator and Authy are popular choices.

- **MFA for Root User**: Always enable MFA for the root user of your AWS account to protect your account from unauthorized access.

Real-World Example: Managing Different Access Levels for Team Members in a Development Environment

Let's consider a development team working on a web application. The team consists of developers, system administrators, and project managers, each of whom needs different access levels to AWS resources.

1. **Developers**:
   - Developers need access to EC2 instances for running and testing the application, and to S3 for uploading and retrieving static assets like images or configuration files.
   - **IAM Group**: Create a **Developers** group with permissions for EC2 and S3 (e.g., **AmazonEC2FullAccess** and **AmazonS3FullAccess**).
   - Developers in this group are granted access to launch, manage, and terminate EC2 instances, but not to manage billing or perform administrative tasks.
2. **System Administrators**:
   - Administrators need full access to EC2 instances, RDS databases, networking configurations, and IAM roles to manage users and security settings.
   - **IAM Group**: Create a **SystemAdmins** group with the **AdministratorAccess** policy attached.

o Administrators can configure security groups, manage IAM roles, and modify instance types as needed.

3. **Project Managers**:

o Project managers only need view-only access to the AWS resources, so they can track project progress and resource usage but cannot make any changes.

o **IAM Group**: Create a **ProjectManagers** group with the **ReadOnlyAccess** policy attached.

o This grants project managers permissions to view EC2 instances, S3 buckets, RDS databases, and CloudWatch metrics but prevents them from making any changes.

How IAM Helps By grouping users into roles based on their responsibilities, you can ensure that each team member has only the permissions necessary to do their job. IAM makes it easy to enforce the principle of least privilege and avoid unintentional or malicious access to sensitive resources.

In this chapter, we've covered how to create and manage users and groups in IAM, define access control using IAM policies, secure your account with Multi-Factor Authentication (MFA), and manage access levels in a development environment. As you continue to build on your AWS knowledge, mastering IAM will be crucial to maintaining a secure and well-organized AWS environment. In the next chapters, we will explore more advanced IAM features and security best practices to further strengthen your AWS infrastructure.

CHAPTER 7

NETWORKING IN AWS - VPC AND SUBNETS

In this chapter, we will explore **Amazon Virtual Private Cloud (VPC)**, the core service that allows you to create isolated networking environments within AWS. VPC is essential for building secure, scalable, and highly available applications in the cloud. We will also cover how to configure subnets, route tables, gateways, security groups, and network access control lists (NACLs) to manage your network infrastructure. A real-world example of setting up a VPC for a secure multi-tier application will tie everything together.

Virtual Private Cloud (VPC): What It Is, How to Set Up VPCs for Isolated Networking

What is VPC? A **Virtual Private Cloud (VPC)** is a logically isolated section of the AWS cloud where you can define and control your virtual network. You can launch AWS resources (such as EC2 instances, RDS databases, etc.) into a VPC, giving you full control over your network topology, including IP address ranges, subnets, route tables, and security settings.

Why Use a VPC? A VPC provides a secure and isolated network environment for your resources. It allows you to:

- **Control IP addressing**: Define your private IP address range using CIDR notation (e.g., 10.0.0.0/16).
- **Subnets**: Divide your VPC into subnets (public, private, or isolated) to segment your application layers.
- **Connectivity**: Control how your resources communicate with each other and the internet (via an Internet Gateway or NAT Gateway).

Steps to Set Up a VPC

1. **Navigate to VPC Dashboard**: From the AWS Management Console, go to **VPC** under the "Networking & Content Delivery" section.
2. **Create a New VPC**:
   - Click **Create VPC**.
   - Enter a **CIDR block** (e.g., `10.0.0.0/16`) to define the address range for your VPC.
   - Choose whether you want to use a **Default VPC** (if you're just getting started) or create a custom VPC for more control.
   - Optionally, select **Tenancy**: Shared or Dedicated (for more isolated hardware).
3. **Create a VPC with Subnets**: You can specify the number of public and private subnets within your VPC.

AWS automatically creates a default **public subnet** for you if you choose the default VPC.

4. **Set Up Internet Gateway**: If you want your VPC to communicate with the internet, attach an **Internet Gateway** (IGW) to the VPC.

Subnets, Route Tables, and Gateways: Configuring Network Components

Subnets

- A **subnet** is a range of IP addresses within your VPC. You can create multiple subnets within a VPC to divide your network for organizational or security purposes.
- **Public Subnet**: A subnet that has access to the internet (via an Internet Gateway).
- **Private Subnet**: A subnet that does not have direct access to the internet. Resources in private subnets typically access the internet via a **NAT Gateway**.
- **Isolated Subnet**: A subnet that is entirely isolated, with no internet access.

Creating Subnets:

1. After creating your VPC, navigate to **Subnets** in the VPC Dashboard.

2. Click **Create Subnet** and provide the following information:

   o **Subnet Name**: Name for the subnet (e.g., `public-subnet` or `private-subnet`).

   o **Availability Zone**: Select an Availability Zone (AZ) to distribute resources across multiple zones for high availability.

   o **CIDR Block**: Define a smaller address range for the subnet (e.g., `10.0.1.0/24`).

Route Tables

- **Route Tables** define how network traffic is directed within a VPC. Every subnet in a VPC must be associated with a route table.

   o **Main Route Table**: Automatically created when you create a VPC.

   o **Custom Route Tables**: You can create custom route tables to control traffic routing for specific subnets.

Setting Up a Route Table:

1. From the VPC Dashboard, click **Route Tables**.
2. Select **Create Route Table**, then configure the route table for the subnets as needed (e.g., route internet-bound traffic from a public subnet via the Internet Gateway).

Gateways

- **Internet Gateway (IGW)**: Connects your VPC to the internet. If you want to enable your resources in public subnets to access the internet, you must attach an IGW to the VPC.
- **NAT Gateway**: Allows instances in private subnets to access the internet, but it does not allow incoming internet traffic to reach those instances.

Creating an Internet Gateway:

1. Go to the **Internet Gateways** section in the VPC Dashboard.
2. Click **Create Internet Gateway**, and then attach it to your VPC.

Security Groups and NACLs: Managing Firewalls and Network Access

Security Groups:

- **Security Groups (SGs)** act as a virtual firewall for EC2 instances to control inbound and outbound traffic.
- SGs are stateful, meaning if you allow incoming traffic, the outgoing traffic will be automatically allowed as well (and vice versa).

Creating and Configuring a Security Group:

1. From the **VPC Dashboard**, navigate to **Security Groups**.

2. Click **Create Security Group**, and configure the inbound and outbound rules for the group (e.g., allow HTTP traffic on port 80 and SSH access on port 22).

3. Attach the security group to your EC2 instances when you launch them or modify an existing instance's security group.

Network Access Control Lists (NACLs):

- **NACLs** are stateless firewalls that control traffic at the subnet level. Unlike security groups, NACLs require you to specify both inbound and outbound rules explicitly.

- NACLs are used to provide an additional layer of security, especially when you want to implement more granular control at the subnet level.

Creating and Configuring a NACL:

1. From the **VPC Dashboard**, navigate to **Network ACLs**.

2. Click **Create Network ACL**, and configure the inbound and outbound rules (e.g., allow HTTP and HTTPS traffic).

3. Associate the NACL with your subnets for the desired network traffic control.

71

Real-World Example: Setting Up a VPC for a Secure Multi-Tier Application

Let's look at how a multi-tier application can be deployed securely using a VPC, involving public and private subnets.

1. **Create a VPC**:
   o First, create a VPC with the CIDR block `10.0.0.0/16`, which will provide ample IP addresses for multiple subnets.

2. **Create Subnets**:
   o Create two **public subnets** (one in each Availability Zone) for the web layer, with CIDR blocks like `10.0.1.0/24` and `10.0.2.0/24`.
   o Create two **private subnets** (again, one in each Availability Zone) for the application and database layers, with CIDR blocks like `10.0.3.0/24` and `10.0.4.0/24`.

3. **Attach an Internet Gateway**:
   o Create and attach an **Internet Gateway** to your VPC to allow internet access for the web layer.

4. **Create Route Tables**:
   o The **public subnets** should have a route table that routes internet traffic (via the Internet Gateway) to the internet.

- o The **private subnets** should have a route table that routes internet traffic through a **NAT Gateway** in the public subnet, allowing instances in private subnets to access the internet for software updates or data synchronization without exposing them to direct internet access.

5. **Security Groups**:
   - o The **web servers** in the public subnet should have a security group allowing inbound traffic on ports 80 (HTTP) and 443 (HTTPS) from the internet.
   - o The **application servers** in the private subnet should only allow inbound traffic from the web servers (on a specific port, such as 8080).
   - o The **database servers** in the private subnet should only allow inbound traffic from the application servers on the relevant database port (e.g., port 3306 for MySQL).

6. **NACLs**:
   - o Set up **NACLs** for additional layer security by controlling access to and from the subnets. For example, the public subnets can allow inbound HTTP/HTTPS traffic, but the private subnets can block all inbound internet traffic except for traffic from the public subnets.

7. **Launch EC2 Instances**:

o Deploy web servers in the public subnets, application servers in the private subnets, and database servers in the private subnets.

By using a VPC and configuring subnets, route tables, gateways, and security settings, you have created a secure, multi-tier architecture where only the web servers are exposed to the internet, and the application and database servers are isolated in private subnets.

In this chapter, we've learned how to set up a **VPC** for isolated networking in AWS, configure **subnets** for different application tiers, manage **security groups** and **NACLs** for network access control, and implement a **secure multi-tier architecture**. These foundational networking components are critical for building scalable, secure, and high-performance applications on AWS. In the following chapters, we will dive deeper into scaling and automating network management for complex AWS environments.

CHAPTER 8

EC2 AUTO SCALING AND LOAD BALANCING

In this chapter, we will dive into the features of **EC2 Auto Scaling** and **Elastic Load Balancing (ELB)**—two powerful tools for building scalable and highly available applications in AWS. Auto Scaling ensures that your infrastructure can handle varying levels of traffic by automatically adjusting the number of EC2 instances. Meanwhile, Elastic Load Balancing distributes incoming traffic across multiple EC2 instances to ensure high availability and fault tolerance. By the end of this chapter, you will understand how to use these tools to scale your web applications effectively based on incoming traffic.

Auto Scaling Groups: How to Automatically Scale EC2 Instances Based on Load

What is Auto Scaling? Auto Scaling allows you to automatically adjust the number of EC2 instances in your application based on demand. It helps you maintain the required performance while minimizing costs by scaling up during periods of high traffic and scaling down when the demand decreases.

How Auto Scaling Works

1. **Auto Scaling Groups (ASG)**: An Auto Scaling group defines a collection of EC2 instances that are managed together. It ensures that the desired number of instances is always running, scaling automatically based on specified conditions.

2. **Scaling Policies**: You can define policies that determine when the Auto Scaling group should add or remove EC2 instances. Policies can be based on:

   o **CPU utilization**: If CPU usage exceeds a certain threshold, Auto Scaling will launch additional instances.

   o **Network traffic**: If network traffic increases, Auto Scaling can scale the number of instances.

   o **Custom metrics**: You can create custom CloudWatch metrics (such as application-specific performance metrics) to trigger scaling.

Steps to Set Up Auto Scaling

1. **Create a Launch Configuration**: A launch configuration defines the EC2 instance type, AMI, key pair, security groups, and other settings for instances that will be part of the Auto Scaling group.

2. **Create an Auto Scaling Group**:

- o Go to the **Auto Scaling** section in the AWS Management Console.
- o Click **Create Auto Scaling Group**.
- o Choose a launch configuration (created earlier), and specify the VPC and subnets where the instances will be launched.
- o Define the desired capacity (minimum, maximum, and desired number of instances) and set scaling policies.

3. **Define Scaling Policies**:

- o Set up scaling policies for both **scale-out** (adding instances) and **scale-in** (removing instances) based on metrics like CPU utilization or network traffic.
- o You can configure **CloudWatch alarms** to trigger these scaling actions.

Best Practices for Auto Scaling

- • **Use metrics to optimize scaling**: Ensure that scaling actions are triggered by appropriate metrics (e.g., CPU, memory, network usage) to balance performance and cost.
- • **Implement cool-down periods**: After scaling in or out, set a cool-down period to prevent excessive scaling due to transient spikes in traffic.

Elastic Load Balancing (ELB): Distributing Incoming Traffic to Multiple Instances

What is Elastic Load Balancing (ELB)? Elastic Load Balancing is a fully managed service that automatically distributes incoming traffic across multiple EC2 instances. ELB helps ensure that no single instance is overwhelmed with traffic, improving fault tolerance and making your application highly available.

Types of Load Balancers in AWS

1. **Application Load Balancer (ALB)**: Ideal for HTTP and HTTPS traffic. It operates at the application layer (Layer 7) and provides advanced routing features, such as URL-based routing and host-based routing. It's ideal for web applications.

2. **Network Load Balancer (NLB)**: Operates at the network layer (Layer 4). NLB is used for high-performance, low-latency traffic, and is ideal for applications that require millions of requests per second, such as IoT or gaming applications.

3. **Classic Load Balancer (CLB)**: The original load balancer for EC2 instances. It supports both Layer 4 and Layer 7 but is less feature-rich than ALB and NLB. AWS recommends using ALB or NLB for new applications.

How ELB Works

1. **Distributes Traffic**: ELB routes incoming requests to the EC2 instances in your Auto Scaling group, based on the configured routing algorithm. It ensures that no single instance is overloaded by distributing traffic evenly.

2. **Health Checks**: ELB performs health checks on your EC2 instances to ensure they are functioning properly. If an instance becomes unhealthy, ELB will automatically stop routing traffic to that instance and route it to healthy ones.

3. **SSL Termination**: For secure web applications, ELB can terminate SSL/TLS connections, offloading the encryption/decryption workload from your EC2 instances.

Setting Up a Load Balancer

1. **Create a Load Balancer**: In the AWS Management Console, go to **EC2** > **Load Balancers** and click **Create Load Balancer**.

2. **Choose the Type of Load Balancer**: Select either **Application Load Balancer (ALB)** or **Network Load Balancer (NLB)** based on your use case.

3. **Configure Listeners**: A listener defines the protocol and port for routing traffic (e.g., HTTP on port 80, HTTPS on port 443).

4. **Configure Target Groups**: Create target groups that consist of EC2 instances that will receive traffic from the load balancer.

5. **Configure Health Checks**: Set up health checks to determine if your EC2 instances are healthy. ELB will automatically stop sending traffic to unhealthy instances.

Best Practices for Load Balancing

- **Use multiple availability zones (AZs)**: Distribute your instances across multiple AZs for higher fault tolerance.

- **Enable sticky sessions**: If your application requires session persistence (e.g., shopping carts in e-commerce), enable sticky sessions, which route requests from the same user to the same instance.

- **Monitor with CloudWatch**: Set up CloudWatch monitoring to track metrics like traffic volume, latency, and the number of healthy/unhealthy instances.

Real-World Example: Scaling a Web Application Based on Incoming Traffic

Let's consider a simple web application for an e-commerce store that sees fluctuating traffic during sales events and promotions. The goal is to automatically scale the application based on incoming traffic to ensure it performs optimally and cost-effectively.

1. **Set Up Auto Scaling**
   - o The web application is hosted on a fleet of EC2 instances within an **Auto Scaling group**. Initially, the Auto Scaling group is configured with a minimum of 2 instances, a maximum of 10 instances, and a desired capacity of 4 instances.
   - o **Scaling Policies** are set up to trigger when the average **CPU utilization** of the EC2 instances exceeds 75%. If this happens, Auto Scaling adds more instances to handle the increased load. Similarly, if CPU utilization drops below 40%, Auto Scaling reduces the number of instances.

2. **Set Up Elastic Load Balancer**
   - o An **Application Load Balancer (ALB)** is configured to distribute incoming web traffic to the EC2 instances in the Auto Scaling group. The ALB listens for HTTP traffic on port 80 and HTTPS traffic on port 443.
   - o The ALB is set to route traffic based on URL paths (e.g., /checkout goes to a set of instances in the checkout service, while /home goes to a set of instances in the product display service).

  o The ALB performs health checks every 30 seconds to ensure that traffic is only routed to healthy EC2 instances.

3. **Automatic Scaling During Traffic Spikes**

  o During a sales event (e.g., Black Friday), traffic to the website spikes significantly. The Auto Scaling group detects the increased CPU utilization and automatically scales the EC2 instances up from 4 to 8 instances to handle the additional load.

  o As traffic decreases after the sale, the Auto Scaling group scales down the number of EC2 instances back to the minimum configuration to save costs.

4. **Fault Tolerance**

  o The application is deployed across multiple Availability Zones (AZs) to ensure high availability. The ALB distributes traffic evenly across the instances in different AZs.

  o If an instance becomes unhealthy (e.g., due to a crash or network failure), the ALB automatically routes traffic to healthy instances, and the Auto Scaling group replaces the failed instance.

By using **Auto Scaling** and **Elastic Load Balancing**, the e-commerce store can handle varying levels of traffic while maintaining high availability and minimizing costs during off-peak times. These features allow the application to scale dynamically based on demand and provide a seamless experience for customers, even during traffic spikes.

In this chapter, we've learned how **Auto Scaling** can automatically adjust the number of EC2 instances based on traffic, how **Elastic Load Balancing (ELB)** distributes incoming traffic to multiple instances for high availability, and how these services can be combined to scale a web application efficiently. These features are essential for ensuring that your applications remain responsive, cost-effective, and reliable in the cloud. In the next chapters, we will explore more advanced features of EC2 and how to optimize your infrastructure for even greater performance.

CHAPTER 9

ELASTIC BEANSTALK - PLATFORM AS A SERVICE (PAAS)

In this chapter, we will explore **AWS Elastic Beanstalk**, a **Platform as a Service (PaaS)** offering that simplifies the deployment and management of applications in AWS. Elastic Beanstalk handles the infrastructure for you—such as provisioning resources, load balancing, scaling, and monitoring—so you can focus on writing code and building your application. By the end of this chapter, you'll understand how to use Elastic Beanstalk to deploy, scale, and manage web applications with ease.

Introduction to Elastic Beanstalk: Simplifying App Deployment

What is Elastic Beanstalk? AWS Elastic Beanstalk is a fully managed service that automatically handles the deployment, scaling, and monitoring of web applications and services. Elastic Beanstalk provides an easy-to-use interface where you can upload your code, and AWS takes care of the rest. This includes managing the underlying infrastructure (e.g., EC2 instances, load balancers, and databases), configuring monitoring tools, and ensuring your application can scale to meet demand.

Elastic Beanstalk supports multiple programming languages and frameworks, such as Node.js, Python, Java, .NET, PHP, Ruby, Go, and Docker, among others. It's a great solution for developers who want to quickly deploy and manage applications without the complexity of managing infrastructure manually.

How Elastic Beanstalk Works

1. **App Deployment**: You upload your application code (such as a ZIP file or Docker container), and Elastic Beanstalk automatically provisions the necessary infrastructure, such as EC2 instances, a load balancer, and a database, if needed.

2. **Automatic Scaling**: Elastic Beanstalk scales your application automatically based on demand, adjusting the number of EC2 instances to handle varying levels of traffic.

3. **Monitoring and Logs**: Elastic Beanstalk provides integrated monitoring, logging, and alerting through **Amazon CloudWatch** and **AWS X-Ray**, giving you insights into your application's performance and issues.

4. **Managed Environment**: Elastic Beanstalk provides a managed environment for your application, including

security patches and updates for the underlying infrastructure.

Deploying Applications: Supported Platforms and Services

Elastic Beanstalk supports a variety of platforms, making it flexible for developers working with different languages and frameworks. Here are some of the most common platforms and services supported:

Supported Platforms

1. **Node.js**: A popular choice for building scalable web applications using JavaScript. Elastic Beanstalk manages the Node.js environment, including web server configuration and dependency management.
2. **Java**: Supports applications running on **Apache Tomcat** or **Java SE**. Java applications can be deployed with minimal configuration, including support for Maven and Gradle.
3. **Python**: Elastic Beanstalk supports **Flask, Django**, and other Python web frameworks, providing a platform for rapid development of Python-based applications.
4. **.NET**: For developers using the .NET framework, Elastic Beanstalk provides an environment for both **ASP.NET** and **ASP.NET Core** applications.

5. **PHP**: Elastic Beanstalk supports popular PHP frameworks, such as **Laravel** and **WordPress**, making it a suitable platform for PHP-based web applications.

6. **Ruby**: Ruby on Rails applications can be deployed with Elastic Beanstalk, simplifying the setup of Ruby environments.

7. **Docker**: Elastic Beanstalk can run applications inside Docker containers, giving you the flexibility to use any technology stack that runs in Docker.

Supported Services

- **RDS** (Relational Database Service): Elastic Beanstalk can automatically integrate with RDS to deploy databases such as MySQL, PostgreSQL, or SQL Server.

- **S3** (Simple Storage Service): Elastic Beanstalk applications can use S3 for static file storage, such as images or documents.

- **SNS** (Simple Notification Service): Elastic Beanstalk can integrate with SNS to send notifications based on application events.

Scaling and Managing Applications: Monitoring and Adjusting Resources

Automatic Scaling Elastic Beanstalk automatically adjusts the number of EC2 instances running your application based on load. This means your application can seamlessly handle traffic spikes without manual intervention. You can configure scaling options like:

1. **Scaling Triggers**: Set thresholds for CPU utilization, memory usage, or other metrics to trigger scaling actions. For example, if CPU usage exceeds 70%, Elastic Beanstalk can scale up the number of instances.

2. **Min/Max Instances**: Define a minimum and maximum number of EC2 instances to ensure that your application has sufficient resources at all times while keeping costs under control.

3. **Load Balancing**: Elastic Beanstalk automatically adds an **Elastic Load Balancer (ELB)** to distribute incoming traffic across your EC2 instances, ensuring high availability and fault tolerance.

Monitoring Your Application Elastic Beanstalk integrates with **Amazon CloudWatch** to provide detailed metrics for monitoring your application. You can monitor metrics such as:

- **CPU Utilization**: Measures how much CPU your EC2 instances are using.

- **Network Traffic**: Shows the amount of incoming and outgoing data.

- **Request Count and Response Time**: Metrics for tracking how many requests your application is handling and how quickly it responds.

Elastic Beanstalk also provides application logs, which can be accessed through the AWS Management Console, the AWS CLI, or directly from the instance itself. These logs can help you debug issues, track performance, and gain insights into how your application is behaving.

Adjusting Resources If your application's needs change, you can adjust the environment by:

- **Modifying Instance Types**: If your app requires more compute power, you can change the EC2 instance type (e.g., from **t2.micro** to **t3.medium**) in your Elastic Beanstalk environment.

- **Increasing Storage**: If your app needs more storage, you can increase the size of the EBS volumes associated with your EC2 instances.

- **Configuring Environment Variables**: You can define environment variables (e.g., database credentials, API keys) directly in the Elastic Beanstalk environment, which are accessible to your application.

Real-World Example: Deploying a Node.js App with Elastic Beanstalk

Let's walk through the process of deploying a **Node.js** application with Elastic Beanstalk.

Step 1: Prepare the Node.js Application Before deploying to Elastic Beanstalk, ensure your Node.js application is ready:

- Your application should have a **package.json** file with the necessary dependencies.
- Ensure that your app listens on the correct port. Elastic Beanstalk expects the app to listen on port 8081 by default, but you can change this if necessary.

Step 2: Create an Elastic Beanstalk Environment

1. Go to the **Elastic Beanstalk Dashboard** in the AWS Management Console.
2. Click **Create a new environment**.
3. Choose **Web Server Environment** and select **Node.js** as the platform.
4. Upload your Node.js application (usually in a ZIP file format) or use **AWS CLI** to deploy the app directly.

5. Elastic Beanstalk automatically provisions EC2 instances, an Elastic Load Balancer, and other required resources.

Step 3: Configure Scaling

1. Define **min** and **max** EC2 instances. For a small app, you might start with 1 instance, but during periods of high traffic, you can scale up to multiple instances.
2. Set up **auto-scaling** triggers based on metrics such as CPU utilization. For example, if CPU utilization exceeds 70%, Elastic Beanstalk will add more EC2 instances.

Step 4: Monitor and Adjust

- After deployment, monitor the health and performance of your application using **CloudWatch metrics** and **Elastic Beanstalk monitoring** tools.
- You can adjust scaling settings if the traffic increases or decreases.

Step 5: Update and Manage the App

- When you need to deploy updates to the Node.js application, simply upload a new version of the app (ZIP file) or use the **AWS CLI** to deploy it.
- Elastic Beanstalk takes care of the deployment, ensuring that traffic is routed to healthy instances while new ones are being launched.

Step 6: Use Logs for Troubleshooting

- If there are any issues with your application, you can access detailed logs directly from the Elastic Beanstalk dashboard. Logs can include information on application errors, performance bottlenecks, and more.

By using Elastic Beanstalk, you've successfully deployed and managed a Node.js application without worrying about infrastructure management. Elastic Beanstalk automatically handles the scaling, monitoring, and load balancing of your application, allowing you to focus on your code and business logic.

In this chapter, we've covered the basics of deploying applications with **Elastic Beanstalk**, how to scale and monitor your application automatically, and how to manage resources through the AWS Management Console. By leveraging Elastic Beanstalk, you can simplify the complexity of deploying web applications, enabling rapid development and reliable scaling. In the following chapters, we will explore more advanced topics such as database integration, security configurations, and troubleshooting with Elastic Beanstalk.

CHAPTER 10

AWS LAMBDA - SERVERLESS COMPUTING

In this chapter, we will explore **AWS Lambda**, a revolutionary service that allows you to run code in response to events without provisioning or managing servers. AWS Lambda is a prime example of **serverless computing**, a model that enables you to focus solely on writing code while AWS takes care of the underlying infrastructure. We will discuss how serverless computing works, how to create and deploy Lambda functions, and how to integrate Lambda with other AWS services to build event-driven architectures. Finally, we will look at a real-world example of how Lambda can be used in a photo-sharing app to process images automatically.

Introduction to Serverless: What Serverless Computing Is and Its Benefits

What is Serverless Computing? Serverless computing is a cloud computing model where the cloud provider (AWS, in this case) manages the infrastructure required to run your code. You no longer need to provision or manage servers; you simply upload your code, and the provider automatically handles the scaling, execution, and infrastructure management.

Key Features of Serverless Computing:

1. **No Server Management**: You don't need to worry about provisioning, scaling, or maintaining servers. AWS Lambda automatically manages the infrastructure for you.
2. **Event-Driven**: Lambda functions are triggered by events such as file uploads to S3, database updates, HTTP requests via API Gateway, or messages from SNS/SQS.
3. **Automatic Scaling**: Lambda automatically scales to handle the number of requests, whether it's a few invocations or thousands per second, with no additional configuration required.
4. **Cost-Efficient**: You pay only for the compute time you use. There are no charges for idle time, and you are billed based on the number of function invocations and the execution duration.
5. **Stateless**: Lambda functions are stateless, meaning each invocation is independent of others. Any state data must be stored in external services (like S3 or DynamoDB).

Benefits of Serverless Computing:

- **Simplified Management**: You don't need to manage servers or worry about patching, scaling, or availability.

- **Cost Efficiency**: With Lambda, you pay only for the execution time of your functions. There's no need to over-provision resources or pay for unused capacity.
- **Faster Development**: Serverless removes infrastructure concerns, enabling developers to focus purely on writing application logic.
- **Scalability**: Lambda scales automatically in response to traffic without manual intervention, ensuring that your application can handle varying loads effortlessly.

Creating Lambda Functions: Writing, Deploying, and Testing Functions

What are AWS Lambda Functions? A **Lambda function** is a small piece of code that runs in response to events. These functions are designed to perform a specific task or set of tasks—such as processing data, handling HTTP requests, or running background jobs.

Writing Lambda Functions Lambda functions can be written in several programming languages, including:

- **Node.js**
- **Python**
- **Java**
- **C#**

- **Go** .
- **Ruby**

Let's go through the steps of creating and deploying a Lambda function in Python:

1. **Go to AWS Lambda Console**:
   o Navigate to **AWS Lambda** in the AWS Management Console.
   o Click **Create function** to begin.
2. **Choose a Function Blueprint or Author from Scratch**:
   o Select **Author from scratch** to write a custom Lambda function.
   o Choose a runtime (e.g., **Python 3.8**).
3. **Write the Lambda Function**:
   o Write the function code in the inline editor provided by AWS Lambda. Here's an example of a basic Lambda function in Python:

```python
def lambda_handler(event, context):
    # Print out the event to see what data is passed to the function
    print(f"Event: {event}")
    return {
        'statusCode': 200,
        'body': 'Hello from Lambda!'
```

}

4. **Configure the Function**:

   o   Set the **function name** (e.g., `MyFirstLambda`).

   o   Adjust the **memory** and **timeout** settings based on the expected function performance.

5. **Deploy the Function**:

   o   Once the code is written and configurations are set, click **Deploy** to make the function live.

Testing Lambda Functions

- **Manual Invocation**: You can manually test your function by creating a test event within the Lambda console. For example, you could test the function with an input like a JSON object.

- **Event Sources**: You can set up event sources (e.g., an S3 upload, API Gateway request, SNS notification) to automatically trigger the Lambda function.

Integrating Lambda with Other AWS Services: Event-Driven Architectures

What is Event-Driven Architecture? An **event-driven architecture** is a software design pattern in which the flow of the application is determined by events (changes in state, messages, etc.). In an event-driven architecture, services like **Lambda** react to events from various AWS services (S3, API Gateway, DynamoDB, etc.).

How Lambda Works with AWS Services:

1. **S3 Events**: Lambda can be triggered when an object is uploaded to an S3 bucket. For example, when a user uploads a photo to S3, Lambda can process that image automatically (e.g., resize or apply filters).

2. **API Gateway**: Lambda functions can be exposed as HTTP endpoints using **Amazon API Gateway**. When an HTTP request is made to the endpoint, API Gateway triggers the corresponding Lambda function to process the request.

3. **SNS and SQS**: Lambda can be triggered by messages from **SNS** (Simple Notification Service) or **SQS** (Simple Queue Service). For example, Lambda can handle background jobs triggered by messages in an SQS queue.

4. **CloudWatch Events**: Lambda functions can be scheduled to run at specific times using **Amazon CloudWatch Events**, similar to cron jobs.

Setting Up Lambda with S3 (Example)

1. In the **S3 console**, create a bucket to store images.

2. In the **Lambda console**, create a function that will process the images. For instance, this function could resize the uploaded images.

3. **Configure the S3 Bucket** to trigger the Lambda function when a new object is uploaded (e.g., images).

4. **Test the integration** by uploading an image to the S3 bucket and watching the Lambda function process the image.

Real-World Example: Using Lambda for Image Processing in a Photo-Sharing App

Let's look at how Lambda can be used in a **photo-sharing app** for processing user-uploaded images.

1. **Application Flow**:
   o **User Uploads an Image**: A user uploads a photo to the photo-sharing app, which stores the image in an S3 bucket.

   o **S3 Event Triggers Lambda**: The S3 bucket is configured to trigger a Lambda function whenever a new photo is uploaded.

   o **Lambda Function Processes the Image**: The Lambda function performs image processing tasks like resizing the image, adding filters, or creating thumbnail previews.

2. **Lambda Function Code**: Here's a simple Python Lambda function that resizes an image using the **Pillow** library (a popular Python image processing library).

```python
from PIL import Image
import boto3
import os

s3 = boto3.client('s3')

def lambda_handler(event, context):
    # Get the bucket name and object key
from the event
    bucket                            =
event['Records'][0]['s3']['bucket']['name
']
    key                               =
event['Records'][0]['s3']['object']['key'
]

    # Download the image from S3
    tmp_file      =        '/tmp/'       +
os.path.basename(key)
    s3.download_file(bucket,          key,
tmp_file)

    # Open the image and resize it
```

```
img = Image.open(tmp_file)
img = img.resize((128, 128))  # Resize
to 128x128

# Save the resized image
resized_key    =    'resized/'    +
os.path.basename(key)
img.save('/tmp/' + resized_key)

# Upload the resized image back to S3
s3.upload_file('/tmp/' + resized_key,
bucket, resized_key)

return {
    'statusCode': 200,
    'body':  f'Image  processed  and
saved as {resized_key}'
}
```

3. **Workflow**:

   o   The user uploads a photo to the **S3 bucket**.

   o   The S3 event triggers the Lambda function, which downloads the image, resizes it, and uploads the resized image back to the S3 bucket in a new folder (e.g., `resized/`).

4. **Cost Efficiency**:

   o   Since Lambda only charges for actual execution time, this is a highly cost-effective way to process images. You pay only for the milliseconds the

101

Lambda function runs, with no need to provision servers for image processing.

5. **Scalability**:

   o   As more users upload images, Lambda automatically scales to handle the increased load, ensuring fast and responsive processing without needing to manage any infrastructure.

In this chapter, we've covered the basics of **AWS Lambda** and **serverless computing**, including how to write and deploy Lambda functions, integrate them with other AWS services for event-driven architectures, and use them for practical applications like image processing in a photo-sharing app. Lambda enables you to focus on building your application logic while AWS handles the scaling and infrastructure. In the next chapters, we'll dive deeper into advanced Lambda use cases and integration patterns for complex applications.

CHAPTER 11

AMAZON RDS - RELATIONAL DATABASE MANAGEMENT

In this chapter, we will explore **Amazon RDS (Relational Database Service)**, a managed database service that simplifies the setup, operation, and scaling of relational databases in the cloud. Amazon RDS supports multiple database engines, including **MySQL, PostgreSQL, MariaDB, Oracle**, and **SQL Server**, allowing you to run your database workloads with minimal administrative overhead. We will discuss how RDS works, how to set up and configure RDS instances, and how to manage backups and replication to ensure data availability and durability. A real-world example will help illustrate how RDS can be used to deploy a MySQL database for an eCommerce platform.

Introduction to RDS: What is RDS, and How Does It Simplify Database Management?

What is Amazon RDS? Amazon RDS is a fully managed relational database service that automates common database tasks, such as:

- **Provisioning**: Automatically creates and configures database instances.
- **Patching**: Manages software patching for database engines.
- **Backups**: RDS handles automatic backups and snapshot management.
- **Scaling**: Automatically scales storage and compute resources.
- **Replication**: Provides support for high availability and read replicas.
- **Monitoring**: Integrates with CloudWatch for monitoring and alerting.

With RDS, AWS takes care of the complex administrative tasks, allowing developers to focus on their application and not the database. It offers a range of benefits, including:

- **Simplified Database Setup**: No need to manually install and configure databases. RDS handles the heavy lifting.
- **Automated Backups**: RDS automatically creates backups and allows point-in-time restores.
- **Scaling**: Easily scale compute and storage resources to meet application demands.
- **Security**: Integrates with AWS security services, such as **IAM** and **VPC**, to secure access to your database.

Supported Database Engines in RDS:

- **MySQL**: One of the most widely used open-source databases.

- **PostgreSQL**: A powerful open-source relational database.

- **MariaDB**: A fork of MySQL, optimized for performance and features.

- **Oracle**: A widely used commercial relational database.

- **SQL Server**: Microsoft's relational database engine.

Setting Up an RDS Instance: Launching, Configuring, and Securing Databases

Launching an RDS Instance To set up an RDS instance, follow these steps:

1. **Navigate to the RDS Dashboard**: From the AWS Management Console, go to **RDS** under the "Databases" section.

2. **Choose a Database Engine**: Select the relational database engine you want to use (e.g., MySQL, PostgreSQL).

3. **Configure Database Instance**:
   - **Instance Class**: Choose the instance size based on your performance needs (e.g., **db.t3.micro** for small workloads or **db.m5.large** for larger production environments).

105

- o **Storage**: Choose the storage type (General Purpose SSD, Provisioned IOPS SSD, or Magnetic) and set the required storage size.
- o **DB Instance Identifier**: Name your RDS instance (e.g., `my-ecommerce-db`).
- o **Master Username and Password**: Set the credentials for the database administrator (DBA) account.

4. **Configure Networking**:
   - o **VPC**: Choose the VPC where your database will reside (this is typically the same VPC your EC2 instances are running in).
   - o **Subnet**: Choose a subnet for the database instance. It's recommended to place RDS instances in private subnets for security.
   - o **Security Group**: Set up security groups to control access to your RDS instance. For example, allow access from your EC2 instances but restrict access from the public internet.

5. **Configure Additional Settings** (Optional):
   - o **Backup**: Enable automated backups and set the retention period (default is 7 days).
   - o **Monitoring**: Enable enhanced monitoring for more detailed performance metrics.

       o **Maintenance Window**: Set the preferred maintenance window for automatic patching and updates.

6. **Launch the Instance**: Once everything is configured, click **Launch DB Instance**.

Securing the Database

- **VPC Security**: Use **VPC** and **Security Groups** to control who can access your RDS instance. For example, you might only allow access from specific IP addresses or from other EC2 instances within the same VPC.

- **Encryption**: Enable encryption at rest to protect sensitive data stored in your RDS instance using **AWS Key Management Service (KMS)**.

- **IAM Roles**: Use IAM roles to grant the RDS instance permissions to access other AWS resources, such as S3 buckets or CloudWatch.

Database Backups and Replication: Ensuring Data Availability and Durability

Automated Backups

- **Backup Frequency**: Amazon RDS automatically backs up your database instance daily, with a retention period ranging from 1 to 35 days.

- **Point-in-Time Recovery**: You can restore your database to any specific point in time within the backup retention period. This is useful for recovering from user errors or application bugs.

- **Manual Snapshots**: In addition to automated backups, you can create manual snapshots of your database at any time. These snapshots are retained until you manually delete them.

Replication for High Availability Amazon RDS offers multiple ways to replicate data for high availability and disaster recovery:

1. **Multi-AZ Deployments**: For production environments, you can enable **Multi-AZ** deployments, which automatically replicate data from your primary RDS instance to a standby instance in another availability zone. This provides automatic failover in case of instance or availability zone failure.

    o **Benefits**: Increased availability, fault tolerance, and automatic failover.

2. **Read Replicas**: You can create **read replicas** of your database for scaling read-heavy workloads. These replicas can be in the same region or a different region.

However, read replicas are only available for MySQL, MariaDB, PostgreSQL, and Aurora.

- o **Benefits**: Offload read queries to replicas, enhancing performance and availability.

3. **Cross-Region Replication**: For disaster recovery, you can set up cross-region replication, ensuring that your database is available in a different AWS region in case of a regional outage.

Real-World Example: Deploying a MySQL Database for an eCommerce Platform

Let's walk through a real-world scenario of deploying a **MySQL database** using RDS for an **eCommerce platform**.

1. **Setup the Database Instance**:
   - o The eCommerce platform needs a MySQL database to store product information, user accounts, and transaction records. The development team decides to use **Amazon RDS** to simplify database management.
   - o They choose **MySQL** as the database engine, selecting an **db.m5.large** instance class for production.

    o   For security, they place the database in a **private subnet** within a **VPC**, ensuring that the database is not directly accessible from the internet.

2. **Database Security**:

    o   The team sets up a **Security Group** that allows only specific EC2 instances (running the application) to access the RDS database. They restrict access to the database from the public internet.

    o   **IAM roles** are used to grant the application permission to read from S3 for product images.

3. **Backup and Replication**:

    o   **Automated Backups** are enabled with a 7-day retention period to ensure data can be recovered if needed.

    o   The team also configures **Multi-AZ** deployment for high availability. This ensures that if the primary database instance fails, RDS automatically switches to the standby instance, minimizing downtime.

4. **Scaling with Read Replicas**:

    o   As the eCommerce platform grows, the team adds **read replicas** to offload read-heavy traffic (e.g., product searches, order queries) from the primary database instance.

o These replicas are deployed in the same region to maintain low-latency access for the application.

5. **Monitoring**:

   o The team uses **CloudWatch** to monitor database performance, tracking metrics like CPU utilization, memory usage, and database connections. They also set up **CloudWatch alarms** to notify the team if resource usage exceeds defined thresholds, prompting them to scale the database.

6. **Database Maintenance**:

   o The team configures an appropriate **maintenance window** during off-peak hours for patching and updates. This minimizes the impact on customers during critical times.

In this chapter, we've explored **Amazon RDS**, a fully managed service that simplifies the process of setting up, operating, and scaling relational databases in the cloud. We've covered how to launch and configure RDS instances, back up and replicate databases for high availability, and secure access to your databases. Finally, through a real-world example, we saw how RDS can be used to deploy a MySQL database for an eCommerce platform. In the next chapters, we will explore advanced database management features, optimization strategies, and how to integrate RDS with other AWS services for enhanced application performance.

CHAPTER 12

AMAZON DYNAMODB - NOSQL DATABASE

In this chapter, we will explore **Amazon DynamoDB**, a fully managed NoSQL database service provided by AWS. DynamoDB is designed to provide high-performance, scalable, and low-latency database solutions for applications that require rapid access to large amounts of data. We will discuss DynamoDB's key features, how to set up and configure tables, and how to manage data consistency and throughput. Additionally, we will go over a real-world example of using DynamoDB for session management in a mobile app.

Introduction to DynamoDB: Key Features and Benefits of NoSQL

What is DynamoDB? Amazon DynamoDB is a managed **NoSQL** database service that provides fast and predictable performance with seamless scalability. Unlike traditional relational databases (SQL), NoSQL databases like DynamoDB do not require a fixed schema or complex join operations, making them ideal for modern applications that deal with large amounts of unstructured or semi-structured data.

Key Features of DynamoDB:

1. **Managed Service**: DynamoDB is fully managed, meaning AWS handles the infrastructure, scaling, replication, and backup tasks. You don't need to worry about provisioning hardware or managing servers.

2. **Scalability**: DynamoDB automatically scales up or down based on your application's throughput and storage requirements. It can handle large amounts of traffic without compromising performance.

3. **High Availability**: DynamoDB is designed for high availability and durability, with data replicated across multiple availability zones within an AWS region.

4. **Low Latency**: DynamoDB is optimized for low-latency access to data, making it suitable for applications that require fast read and write operations.

5. **Flexible Data Model**: DynamoDB uses a **key-value** and **document** data model, making it ideal for use cases like storing user profiles, shopping carts, logs, and session data.

6. **Integrated with AWS Ecosystem**: DynamoDB integrates seamlessly with other AWS services such as Lambda, API Gateway, CloudWatch, and more, making it easy to build event-driven architectures.

Benefits of NoSQL with DynamoDB:

- **Schema-less Design**: You can store data without defining a rigid schema. Each item (record) in a DynamoDB table can have different attributes, which is ideal for applications that need flexibility in data storage.

- **Performance at Scale**: DynamoDB can handle large amounts of data and traffic, automatically adjusting its resources to ensure fast response times.

- **Serverless**: DynamoDB is a serverless database, which means you don't need to manage or provision servers. You pay only for the resources you consume, reducing costs and operational complexity.

Setting Up DynamoDB: Creating Tables, Configuring Indexes, and Writing Data

Creating DynamoDB Tables To begin using DynamoDB, you first need to create a table. A DynamoDB table consists of a set of items (records), and each item has a primary key that uniquely identifies it.

1. **Go to the DynamoDB Console**: Navigate to **DynamoDB** in the AWS Management Console.

2. **Create a Table**:
   - **Table Name**: Provide a unique name for your table.

- o **Primary Key**: DynamoDB tables require a primary key. The primary key can be one of the following:
  - **Partition Key**: A single attribute (e.g., `UserID` or `ProductID`).
  - **Partition Key + Sort Key**: A composite key where the partition key is combined with a sort key to allow more complex queries (e.g., `UserID` + `Timestamp`).
- o **Provisioned or On-Demand Capacity**: You can choose between provisioned (manual throughput control) or on-demand (automatic scaling) capacity modes for your table.

3. **Configure Secondary Indexes (Optional)**: If you need to query data in ways other than the primary key, you can create **Global Secondary Indexes (GSI)** or **Local Secondary Indexes (LSI)**. GSIs allow you to query on non-key attributes, while LSIs allow you to query on non-primary key attributes while using the same partition key.

4. **Set Table Options**: Configure optional settings like **Time to Live (TTL)**, which automatically deletes items after a specified period, and **Stream Settings** to enable data streams for event-driven applications.

Example: Creating a Table

json

```
{
  "TableName": "Users",
  "KeySchema": [
    { "AttributeName": "UserID", "KeyType":
"HASH" },
    { "AttributeName": "Email", "KeyType":
"RANGE" }
  ],
  "AttributeDefinitions": [
    {        "AttributeName":        "UserID",
"AttributeType": "S" },
    { "AttributeName": "Email", "AttributeType":
"S" }
  ],
  "ProvisionedThroughput": {
    "ReadCapacityUnits": 5,
    "WriteCapacityUnits": 5
  }
}
```

Writing Data to DynamoDB Once your table is set up, you can start adding items to it. Each item is a set of key-value pairs. Here's how you can insert data using the AWS SDK:

1. **Insert an Item using the AWS SDK (e.g., Python)**

```python

import boto3
```

```
# Create a DynamoDB resource
dynamodb = boto3.resource('dynamodb')

# Reference the Users table
table = dynamodb.Table('Users')

# Insert an item
response = table.put_item(
    Item={
        'UserID': '12345',
        'Email': 'user@example.com',
        'Name': 'John Doe',
        'Age': 30,
        'Address': '1234 Elm St, Some City,
USA'
    }
)

print("PutItem succeeded:", response)
```

Best Practices for Table Configuration

- **Use Simple Keys**: For efficient querying, keep the primary key as simple as possible.
- **Avoid Hot Keys**: When designing your partition key, avoid selecting a key that may lead to "hot keys" (i.e., partitioning a table in such a way that certain partitions are accessed far more frequently than others).

- **Design for Scaling**: DynamoDB can scale automatically, but it's still important to design your table to handle large amounts of data efficiently, especially when using provisioned throughput.

Data Consistency and Scaling: Managing Throughput and Consistency

Consistency Models in DynamoDB DynamoDB offers two consistency models for reading data:

1. **Eventual Consistency**: In this model, reads may not reflect the most recent writes immediately. This model is faster and reduces costs but may return stale data temporarily.
2. **Strong Consistency**: With strong consistency, reads always return the most up-to-date data, but this comes at the cost of slightly higher latency and higher read throughput.

Managing Throughput When configuring DynamoDB tables, you can specify the **read capacity units** (RCUs) and **write capacity units** (WCUs) for provisioned tables:

- **Read Capacity Units (RCUs)**: Define how many strongly consistent reads (or eventually consistent reads) can be performed per second.
- **Write Capacity Units (WCUs)**: Define how many writes per second the table can handle.

If you choose **on-demand** capacity, DynamoDB will automatically scale your table's throughput based on demand, so you don't have to worry about managing capacity manually.

Scaling DynamoDB

- **Auto Scaling**: You can enable auto scaling to automatically adjust the read and write capacity based on your application's traffic. This ensures your table has sufficient capacity to handle spikes in usage while optimizing costs during periods of low activity.
- **Global Tables**: DynamoDB also offers **Global Tables**, allowing you to replicate tables across multiple AWS regions for increased availability and fault tolerance.

Real-World Example: Using DynamoDB for Session Management in a Mobile App

Let's consider a **mobile app** that needs to manage user sessions. DynamoDB is a great choice for session management because of its low-latency performance and ability to handle large amounts of data efficiently.

1. **Create a Table for Sessions**: The table will have a **SessionID** as the partition key and **UserID** as the sort key. This allows the app to track sessions by user and quickly retrieve session data using the session ID.

   Table Structure:

   - **SessionID (HASH key)**: Unique identifier for each session.
   - **UserID (RANGE key)**: The user associated with the session.
   - **Timestamp**: The time when the session was created.
   - **SessionData**: The session information (e.g., user preferences, authentication tokens).

2. **Storing Session Data**: When a user logs in, the app generates a unique **SessionID** and stores session data in DynamoDB.

```python
python

session_data = {
    'SessionID': 'session_12345',
    'UserID': 'user_123',
    'Timestamp': '2022-10-01T10:00:00Z',
```

```
'SessionData': {
    'authToken': 'abc123',
    'preferences': {'theme': 'dark',
'language': 'en'}
    }
}


response                        =
table.put_item(Item=session_data)
```

3. **Retrieving Session Data**: When the app needs to fetch session data, it can use the **SessionID** to retrieve the session record:

```python
python
```

```
response                        =
table.get_item(Key={'SessionID':
'session_12345', 'UserID': 'user_123'})
session_data = response.get('Item')
print(session_data)
```

4. **Expiration**: DynamoDB's **Time to Live (TTL)** feature can automatically delete expired session data. You can configure TTL to delete sessions that have been inactive for a certain period, reducing storage costs.

5. **Scaling**: As the app grows and more users interact with it, DynamoDB automatically scales to handle increased

session data traffic, without requiring manual intervention.

In this chapter, we've learned about **Amazon DynamoDB**, a powerful NoSQL database that simplifies data management and scales automatically to meet application needs. We covered how to set up DynamoDB tables, manage throughput and consistency, and integrate DynamoDB into applications. By using DynamoDB for session management in a mobile app, we demonstrated how its features can help handle large amounts of user data with low latency and high availability. In the next chapters, we will explore advanced features like **global tables**, **streams**, and **DynamoDB transactions** for even more powerful use cases.

CHAPTER 13

AMAZON SQS AND SNS - MESSAGING AND NOTIFICATIONS

In this chapter, we will explore **Amazon SQS (Simple Queue Service) and Amazon SNS (Simple Notification Service)**, two core messaging services provided by AWS that allow you to build decoupled, event-driven architectures. These services enable you to manage communication between distributed components in your application without the need for direct connections. We will discuss how SQS and SNS work, how to set them up, and a real-world example of using SQS to manage order processing in an eCommerce app.

Introduction to SQS (Simple Queue Service): Queue Management for Decoupled Services

What is SQS? Amazon **SQS** is a fully managed message queuing service that allows you to decouple and scale microservices, distributed systems, and serverless applications. It enables you to send, store, and receive messages between different components of your application in a reliable and scalable manner.

How SQS Works SQS helps in decoupling different parts of an application by acting as a buffer between producers and consumers. When a producer (such as an application component or service) sends a message, it is stored in an **SQS queue**. Consumers (such as other services or microservices) can then retrieve and process these messages at their own pace.

Key Features of SQS:

1. **Decoupling**: Services can operate independently and communicate via messages, allowing you to scale and modify them without impacting other components.

2. **Reliable**: SQS ensures that messages are delivered at least once, and in the case of network issues or component failures, it can retry message delivery.

3. **Scalable**: SQS automatically scales to handle large amounts of messages, making it suitable for high-throughput systems.

4. **Fully Managed**: AWS manages the infrastructure, so you don't need to worry about setting up and maintaining servers.

5. **Types of Queues**:
   - **Standard Queue**: Provides at-least-once delivery and is best for applications where the order of messages is not critical.
   - **FIFO Queue (First-In-First-Out)**: Ensures exactly-once message delivery and guarantees

the order of messages. It's ideal for applications where the sequence of events is important (e.g., order processing).

Setting Up an SQS Queue

1. **Go to the SQS Dashboard** in the AWS Management Console.

2. **Click "Create Queue"** to create a new queue.

3. **Choose Queue Type**: Select either **Standard Queue** or **FIFO Queue** based on your application's needs.

4. **Configure Queue Settings**:
   o   Set the **queue name**.
   o   Configure the **message retention period**, which defines how long messages stay in the queue.
   o   Set the **visibility timeout** to specify how long a message remains invisible to other consumers once it's being processed.

5. **Access Control**: Set the **permissions** to control who can send and receive messages from the queue.

Best Practices for SQS

• **Set an appropriate message retention period** to avoid unnecessary storage costs.

- **Use dead-letter queues** (DLQs) for messages that can't be successfully processed, ensuring that failed messages don't get lost.
- **Optimize polling** by configuring consumers to poll the queue in an efficient manner (e.g., by adjusting the wait time for long polling).

Introduction to SNS (Simple Notification Service): Sending Notifications

What is SNS? Amazon **SNS** is a fully managed pub/sub messaging service that allows you to send messages (notifications) to a large number of recipients, including application endpoints, email, SMS, and mobile devices. It allows for event-driven architectures and is typically used for broadcasting messages to multiple consumers or triggering actions in multiple systems at once.

How SNS Works SNS allows you to create **topics**, which are logical channels that you can use to broadcast messages to multiple subscribers. Each subscriber can be an endpoint such as an SQS queue, an HTTP endpoint, an email address, or even a Lambda function. When a message is published to a topic, it's automatically delivered to all subscribed endpoints.

Key Features of SNS:

127

1. **Pub/Sub Messaging**: SNS allows you to broadcast messages to multiple subscribers, making it ideal for use cases such as alerting, notifications, and event-driven workflows.

2. **Multiple Protocols**: SNS supports various message delivery protocols, such as HTTP/HTTPS, email, SMS, Lambda functions, and even SQS queues.

3. **Fan-out**: SNS enables message fan-out, allowing a single message to trigger multiple downstream processes (e.g., sending an email and an SMS simultaneously).

4. **Mobile Push Notifications**: SNS integrates with mobile push notification services such as **Amazon SNS Mobile Push** for sending notifications to iOS, Android, and Fire OS devices.

Setting Up an SNS Topic

1. **Go to the SNS Dashboard** in the AWS Management Console.

2. **Click "Create Topic"** to create a new topic.

3. **Choose a Topic Type**: Select either **Standard** or **FIFO** based on your requirements.

4. **Configure Topic Settings**:
   - Set the **topic name**.
   - Configure **access control policies** to manage who can publish messages to the topic.

5. **Create Subscriptions**: After creating the topic, you can add subscribers (e.g., an SQS queue, an email address, or a Lambda function). SNS will send messages to all subscribers whenever a message is published to the topic.

Best Practices for SNS

- **Use Topics for Efficient Message Delivery**: SNS topics allow you to send messages to many recipients without the need to address each one individually.
- **Use Delivery Policies**: Configure retry policies and set up dead-letter queues for failed deliveries.
- **Secure Your Topics**: Use IAM policies and access control lists (ACLs) to control who can publish or subscribe to your topics.

Real-World Example: Using SQS to Manage Order Processing in an eCommerce App

Let's walk through how **SQS** can be used in an **eCommerce app** to manage the order processing workflow.

Scenario: When a customer places an order, the eCommerce platform needs to process payment, update inventory, and send confirmation emails. These tasks are independent, and you want to decouple them so that each task can be handled asynchronously without overloading the system.

1. **Order Placement**:
   - ○ When a customer places an order, the application triggers an event and places an order message in the **SQS queue**. The message contains all the order details (e.g., customer information, items, payment status).

2. **Processing the Order**:
   - ○ **Order Service**: The order message is retrieved from the SQS queue by the order service, which handles the payment processing.
   - ○ **Inventory Service**: Once payment is confirmed, the order service publishes a new message to a second queue that the **inventory service** listens to. This service then updates the inventory.
   - ○ **Notification Service**: Finally, the order service sends a notification message to an **SNS topic**, which triggers an **email** and **SMS notification** to the customer, confirming the order.

3. **Scalability**:
   - ○ **Auto-Scaling**: If the order volume increases (e.g., during a sale), the system can automatically scale the number of workers (EC2 instances or Lambda functions) processing the SQS queues, ensuring that the processing continues smoothly.

4. **Fault Tolerance**:

   o **Dead-Letter Queues (DLQ)**: If an order fails to process (e.g., due to a payment issue), the message can be sent to a DLQ, allowing the development team to inspect and resolve the issue without losing data.

5. **Event-Driven Workflow**:

   o **SNS Integration**: By using SNS for notifications, the system can easily send updates to different services (such as an admin dashboard or customer service) or trigger other workflows, such as generating invoices or shipping requests.

Benefits of Using SQS and SNS in this Scenario:

- **Decoupling**: Each service (payment processing, inventory management, notifications) operates independently, which makes the system more scalable and easier to maintain.

- **Asynchronous Processing**: The use of SQS queues allows the platform to handle multiple tasks simultaneously, reducing the risk of overloading the system during peak times (e.g., sales).

- **Flexibility and Scalability**: The system can automatically scale the number of workers processing orders based on demand, ensuring that order processing remains efficient even during traffic spikes.

In this chapter, we've learned about **Amazon SQS** and **SNS**, two powerful messaging services that allow you to build decoupled, event-driven architectures. We covered how to set up and configure both services, how to integrate them for seamless communication between distributed components, and provided a real-world example of using SQS for managing order processing in an eCommerce app. These services provide the foundation for building scalable, fault-tolerant applications that can efficiently process large volumes of data and events. In the next chapters, we will explore more advanced features of SQS and SNS, including message filtering, dead-letter queues, and integrating them with AWS Lambda for serverless applications.

CHAPTER 14

AMAZON CLOUDFRONT - CONTENT DELIVERY NETWORK (CDN)

In this chapter, we will explore **Amazon CloudFront**, AWS's Content Delivery Network (CDN) service. CloudFront enables fast delivery of content (like web pages, images, videos, and other assets) to users worldwide by leveraging a network of edge locations. This chapter will cover what a CDN is, why it's important for web applications, how to set up and configure CloudFront distributions, and provide a real-world example of using CloudFront to speed up website delivery for global users.

Introduction to CloudFront: What is a CDN and Why It's Important?

What is a Content Delivery Network (CDN)? A **Content Delivery Network (CDN)** is a system of distributed servers (called **edge locations**) that deliver content (e.g., images, videos, HTML, CSS, JavaScript files) to users based on their geographic location. The primary goal of a CDN is to reduce latency by serving content from the nearest available server, improving load times and user experience.

How Does CloudFront Work? Amazon **CloudFront** is AWS's global CDN service that delivers static and dynamic content to users with low latency and high transfer speeds. CloudFront caches copies of your content in **edge locations** worldwide. When a user requests content, CloudFront routes the request to the nearest edge location to provide the content as quickly as possible.

For example, if you have a website hosted in the US, and a user in Europe accesses your site, CloudFront will serve the content from the nearest European edge location instead of your primary server, reducing load times and improving performance.

Why Use a CDN?

1. **Improved Performance**: CDNs reduce latency by serving content from edge locations close to the user, improving website load times.
2. **Scalability**: CDNs handle high traffic spikes by offloading traffic from your origin server, ensuring your website performs well during periods of high demand (e.g., product launches, promotions).
3. **Global Reach**: With multiple edge locations worldwide, CDNs allow you to provide a consistent experience to users across the globe.

4. **Reliability**: CDNs enhance fault tolerance by providing backup locations in case of server or network failures.

5. **Security**: CDNs like CloudFront provide security features like **SSL/TLS encryption** and **DDoS protection** to safeguard your content.

Setting Up CloudFront Distributions: Configuring Edge Locations for Faster Content Delivery

Creating a CloudFront Distribution A **CloudFront distribution** is the configuration that tells CloudFront how to deliver your content. There are two types of distributions you can create:

1. **Web Distribution**: This is used for delivering static content (e.g., images, JavaScript, CSS) and dynamic content (e.g., API responses).

2. **RTMP Distribution**: This is used for streaming media using the **Adobe Flash Media Server** or **RTMP** protocol.

To set up a **Web Distribution** in CloudFront, follow these steps:

1. **Go to the CloudFront Console**:
   - Open the **AWS Management Console**, navigate to **CloudFront**, and click **Create Distribution**.

2. **Choose Web Distribution**:
   o Select **Web** for the distribution type, then click **Get Started**.

3. **Configure the Origin**:
   o **Origin Domain Name**: Enter the domain of the origin server (e.g., your S3 bucket URL or an HTTP server URL). This is where CloudFront will pull content from.
   o **Origin ID**: Give a unique identifier to the origin.
   o **Origin Protocol Policy**: Choose the protocol for communication between CloudFront and your origin (HTTP or HTTPS).

4. **Configure Cache Settings**:
   o **Cache Behavior**: Define how CloudFront caches your content. For example, you can specify whether the cache should be based on the query string, headers, and cookies.
   o **Viewer Protocol Policy**: Choose whether CloudFront should allow **HTTP**, **HTTPS**, or both for serving content.
   o **TTL (Time to Live)**: Set how long CloudFront should cache content before rechecking the origin.

5. **Configure Distribution Settings**:

- o **Alternate Domain Names (CNAMEs)**: If you want to use custom domain names (e.g., cdn.example.com), you can add them here.
- o **SSL Certificate**: For secure HTTPS delivery, select an SSL certificate for your domain.

6. **Enable Logging**:
   - o CloudFront can generate log files of all requests made to your distribution, which can be useful for analyzing traffic patterns or debugging issues.

7. **Create Distribution**:
   - o After configuring all settings, click **Create Distribution**. CloudFront will take a few minutes to deploy your distribution across its global network of edge locations.

Configuring Edge Locations Once your distribution is created, CloudFront will automatically use its **edge locations** to cache and serve content based on where the user is located. You don't need to manually configure each edge location; CloudFront will intelligently choose the nearest one based on the user's request.

You can view the locations where CloudFront has edge servers by looking at the **Region** column in the CloudFront distribution details.

Real-World Example: Speeding Up Website Delivery for Global Users Using CloudFront

Let's consider a **global eCommerce website** with customers from around the world. The website is hosted in AWS and stores its assets (images, product data, static content) in an **S3 bucket**. To provide a fast and responsive experience to users in different regions, CloudFront is used to cache and deliver content.

1. Setting Up the S3 Bucket as the Origin

- The website's static content (images, product descriptions, JavaScript files) is stored in an **S3 bucket**. CloudFront is configured to use this S3 bucket as the **origin** for the distribution.

2. Configuring the CloudFront Distribution

- A **Web Distribution** is created, with the S3 bucket as the origin.
- The **Origin Protocol Policy** is set to **HTTPS**, ensuring that content is securely delivered from the S3 bucket to CloudFront.
- **Cache Behavior** is configured to cache product images for a longer duration (e.g., 1 hour) while caching dynamic content like user reviews for a shorter period.

- **SSL/TLS encryption** is enabled for secure HTTPS delivery, and a custom domain (cdn.myshop.com) is used with CloudFront.

3. Global Reach and Faster Delivery

- CloudFront has **edge locations** all over the world. For example, users in the US will be served from edge locations in the US, while users in Europe will receive content from European edge locations.
- This significantly reduces latency, as the content is delivered from the nearest edge location rather than the origin server in the AWS region.

4. Automatic Caching and Updates

- When a customer in Asia accesses the site, CloudFront fetches content from the nearest edge location. If it's the first time the content is requested, CloudFront fetches it from the **S3 bucket**.
- If the content is updated, such as when new product images are added to the S3 bucket, CloudFront automatically invalidates its cache, ensuring users receive the latest content without delay.

5. Cost Savings and Performance Monitoring

- CloudFront caches frequently accessed content, reducing the load on the origin server (S3). This minimizes data transfer costs and reduces the need for large-scale backend servers.
- CloudWatch is used to monitor the performance of the CloudFront distribution. Metrics like **cache hit ratio**, **latency**, and **request counts** are monitored to ensure that users around the world are receiving fast, responsive service.

Benefits in this Example:

- **Faster Content Delivery**: Users experience faster page load times because content is served from the nearest edge location.
- **Scalability**: CloudFront automatically scales to handle traffic spikes, such as during sales events or promotions.
- **Reliability**: The eCommerce platform benefits from increased availability, as CloudFront's edge locations are distributed across multiple regions, ensuring continuous service even if one region experiences issues.
- **Cost Efficiency**: By caching content at edge locations, CloudFront reduces the number of requests to the origin server, which leads to lower data transfer costs.

In this chapter, we've learned about **Amazon CloudFront** and how it helps speed up content delivery by leveraging a global network of edge locations. We've discussed how to configure a CloudFront distribution for your website and how it helps improve performance for global users. The real-world example of using CloudFront to speed up website delivery for an eCommerce platform demonstrated how to efficiently serve static and dynamic content to users worldwide while reducing latency and costs. In the next chapters, we will explore advanced CloudFront configurations, including custom cache behaviors, Lambda@Edge, and more.

CHAPTER 15

AWS CLOUDFORMATION - INFRASTRUCTURE AS CODE

In this chapter, we will explore **AWS CloudFormation**, a powerful service that enables you to define and deploy your AWS infrastructure using code. This is known as **Infrastructure as Code (IaC)**, which allows you to manage and provision AWS resources in a consistent, automated, and repeatable way. CloudFormation simplifies infrastructure management by providing a declarative approach to resource provisioning, ensuring that your infrastructure is always deployed the same way, no matter the environment. We will discuss the concept of IaC, how to create CloudFormation templates, how to deploy and manage stacks, and a real-world example of automating the deployment of a multi-tier architecture.

Introduction to CloudFormation: What is Infrastructure as Code (IaC)?

What is Infrastructure as Code (IaC)? Infrastructure as Code (IaC) is the practice of managing and provisioning infrastructure through machine-readable configuration files rather than through manual processes. IaC allows for automation, consistency, and version control of infrastructure, which is particularly useful in cloud environments like AWS where you need to deploy resources at scale.

Key Benefits of IaC:

1. **Automation**: Infrastructure deployment is automated, which reduces human error and ensures consistency across environments.

2. **Version Control**: Infrastructure code can be versioned in the same way as application code, allowing for easy tracking of changes.

3. **Reusability**: Infrastructure code can be reused across multiple environments, ensuring that the same configurations are applied across development, staging, and production environments.

4. **Consistency**: By defining infrastructure in code, you eliminate the risk of configuration drift between environments.

5. **Scalability**: IaC allows you to easily scale your infrastructure up or down by adjusting the code, making it more flexible and adaptable.

AWS CloudFormation Overview AWS CloudFormation is a service that enables you to define AWS infrastructure resources (such as EC2 instances, VPCs, and databases) in a **template**

written in JSON or YAML format. Once the template is defined, CloudFormation can automatically provision and configure these resources in the specified AWS account.

- **Declarative Model**: With CloudFormation, you describe the desired state of your infrastructure (e.g., "I want 3 EC2 instances in a specific VPC"), and CloudFormation ensures that the infrastructure matches that state.
- **Automated Resource Management**: CloudFormation handles resource dependencies, meaning that it automatically provisions resources in the correct order and manages any dependencies between resources.

Creating CloudFormation Templates: Defining Resources Programmatically

What is a CloudFormation Template? A **CloudFormation template** is a JSON or YAML file that describes the resources and their configurations. The template defines AWS resources such as EC2 instances, VPCs, security groups, and other infrastructure components. CloudFormation then reads the template to provision and configure the resources automatically.

A CloudFormation template consists of the following main sections:

1. **Resources**: This is the core section of the template, where you define the AWS resources to be provisioned (e.g., EC2 instances, S3 buckets).

2. **Parameters**: These are optional values that you can pass to the template at runtime, allowing for more flexible templates.

3. **Outputs**: This section allows you to output information about the resources created, such as the IP address of an EC2 instance.

4. **Mappings**: This allows you to define fixed values that can be used for conditional creation of resources.

5. **Conditions**: You can use conditions to determine whether certain resources or properties are created, based on input parameters.

6. **Metadata**: This section is used for defining additional information about the template, such as for use with other services or for organizing resources.

7. **Transform**: For advanced features, you can use the `AWS::CloudFormation::Interface` and other macros to define complex resources and templates.

Example CloudFormation Template (YAML) Here's a basic example of a CloudFormation template that creates an EC2 instance:

```
yaml
```

```
AWSTemplateFormatVersion: '2010-09-09'
Resources:
  MyEC2Instance:
    Type: 'AWS::EC2::Instance'
    Properties:
      InstanceType: t2.micro
      ImageId: ami-0c55b159cbfafe1f0
      KeyName: my-key-pair
      SecurityGroups:
        - my-security-group
```

In this example:

- **AWSTemplateFormatVersion** specifies the version of the CloudFormation template.

- **Resources** defines the resources to be created—in this case, an EC2 instance with a specific instance type and AMI ID.

- The **InstanceType** is set to t2.micro, which is a lightweight instance type suitable for small workloads.

Deploying and Managing Stacks: Automated Infrastructure Management

What is a CloudFormation Stack? A **CloudFormation Stack** is a collection of AWS resources that are managed as a single unit. When you create a stack, CloudFormation provisions the

146

resources defined in the template. You can manage, update, or delete all resources in the stack with a single operation.

Creating a Stack:

1. **Go to the CloudFormation Console** in the AWS Management Console.
2. **Create a New Stack** by clicking **Create Stack**.
3. **Upload or Specify a Template**: You can upload a CloudFormation template file (either JSON or YAML) or provide a URL to an existing template.
4. **Specify Parameters**: If your template includes parameters, CloudFormation will prompt you to specify the values for those parameters.
5. **Review and Create the Stack**: After reviewing your settings, click **Create Stack**. CloudFormation will then provision and configure the resources as described in your template.

Managing Stacks:

- **Updating Stacks**: If you need to make changes to the infrastructure, you can update the CloudFormation stack by modifying the template and then applying the changes. CloudFormation automatically handles resource replacements, additions, or deletions as needed.

- **Stack Deletion**: When you no longer need the resources, you can delete the entire stack, and CloudFormation will automatically clean up all associated resources.

Stack Outputs: After a stack is created, you can view its outputs (e.g., EC2 instance IDs, S3 bucket names) directly from the CloudFormation console. This allows you to reference resources created by CloudFormation in other parts of your application.

Real-World Example: Automating the Deployment of a Multi-Tier Architecture

Let's consider a **multi-tier web application** for an eCommerce platform, consisting of:

1. **Web Tier**: A set of EC2 instances running the web application.
2. **Application Tier**: EC2 instances that handle business logic and application processing.
3. **Database Tier**: An RDS instance for storing customer and order data.

Step 1: Define the CloudFormation Template We will create a CloudFormation template that deploys a complete multi-tier architecture, including:

- A VPC with public and private subnets.

148

- EC2 instances in the public subnet for the web tier.
- EC2 instances in the private subnet for the application tier.
- An RDS instance in the private subnet for the database.

Example Template (YAML):

yaml

```
AWSTemplateFormatVersion: '2010-09-09'
Resources:
  MyVPC:
    Type: 'AWS::EC2::VPC'
    Properties:
      CidrBlock: '10.0.0.0/16'

  MyWebSubnet:
    Type: 'AWS::EC2::Subnet'
    Properties:
      VpcId: !Ref MyVPC
      CidrBlock: '10.0.1.0/24'
      AvailabilityZone: 'us-west-2a'

  MyAppSubnet:
    Type: 'AWS::EC2::Subnet'
    Properties:
      VpcId: !Ref MyVPC
      CidrBlock: '10.0.2.0/24'
      AvailabilityZone: 'us-west-2a'
```

```yaml
WebServer:
  Type: 'AWS::EC2::Instance'
  Properties:
    InstanceType: 't2.micro'
    ImageId: 'ami-0c55b159cbfafe1f0'
    SubnetId: !Ref MyWebSubnet

AppServer:
  Type: 'AWS::EC2::Instance'
  Properties:
    InstanceType: 't2.micro'
    ImageId: 'ami-0c55b159cbfafe1f0'
    SubnetId: !Ref MyAppSubnet

MyRDSInstance:
  Type: 'AWS::RDS::DBInstance'
  Properties:
    DBInstanceClass: 'db.t2.micro'
    Engine: 'MySQL'
    MasterUsername: 'admin'
    MasterUserPassword: 'password'
    DBName: 'ecommerce_db'
    AllocatedStorage: 20
    VPCSecurityGroups:
      - !Ref MySecurityGroup
    DBSubnetGroupName: !Ref MyDBSubnetGroup

MySecurityGroup:
```

```
Type: 'AWS::EC2::SecurityGroup'
Properties:
   GroupDescription: 'Allow web and app server
traffic'
      SecurityGroupIngress:
         - IpProtocol: 'tcp'
           FromPort: '80'
           ToPort: '80'
           CidrIp: '0.0.0.0/0'
         - IpProtocol: 'tcp'
           FromPort: '3306'
           ToPort: '3306'
           CidrIp: '10.0.0.0/16'
```

Step 2: Launch the Stack

- Upload the template to the **CloudFormation Console** and create a stack.
- CloudFormation will automatically provision the VPC, subnets, EC2 instances, and RDS database as specified in the template.

Step 3: Monitor and Update the Stack

- You can monitor the stack's progress via the CloudFormation Console. Once the stack is deployed, you can access the EC2 instances and RDS instance.

151

- If the application requires changes, you can modify the CloudFormation template and update the stack, ensuring that the infrastructure changes are applied automatically.

Benefits of Using CloudFormation in This Example:

- **Consistency**: The application's infrastructure is defined as code, ensuring that the setup is consistent across different environments (e.g., development, staging, production).
- **Automation**: Infrastructure provisioning and configuration are automated, reducing manual setup errors.
- **Scalability**: The template can easily be modified to add more instances or services as the application grows.
- **Version Control**: The CloudFormation template can be stored in version control systems, allowing you to track changes to the infrastructure over time.

In this chapter, we've explored **AWS CloudFormation**, a powerful service for managing infrastructure as code. We've discussed how to create and manage CloudFormation templates, deploy and manage stacks, and automate the deployment of a multi-tier architecture. With CloudFormation, you can define your infrastructure programmatically, improving consistency, scalability, and automation. In the next chapters, we will delve into advanced CloudFormation features, such as StackSets, nested stacks, and custom resources, for even more sophisticated infrastructure management.

CHAPTER 16

AMAZON ELASTIC FILE SYSTEM (EFS)

In this chapter, we will explore **Amazon Elastic File System (EFS)**, a fully managed, scalable file storage service that allows you to create and manage file systems in the cloud. EFS is designed for use with Amazon EC2 instances and other AWS services, providing shared file storage for applications and workloads that require a scalable and highly available storage solution. We will discuss how EFS works, how to set it up and mount it on EC2 instances, and a real-world example of using EFS for shared storage across multiple instances in a web application.

Introduction to EFS: Scalable File Storage for AWS

What is Amazon EFS? Amazon **Elastic File System (EFS)** is a scalable and fully managed file storage service that provides a simple, serverless, cloud-native NFS (Network File System) file system. EFS allows you to store and access data across multiple EC2 instances simultaneously, enabling shared access to files in real time.

Unlike traditional file systems, EFS automatically scales as you add or remove data, and it is designed to work seamlessly with a variety of AWS services and on-premises resources. EFS provides the performance and durability needed for workloads like web applications, content management systems, big data analytics, and machine learning.

Key Features of Amazon EFS:

1. **Scalability**: EFS automatically scales up or down based on the amount of data you store, meaning there's no need to provision or manage capacity manually.

2. **Shared Access**: Multiple EC2 instances or AWS services can access the same EFS file system simultaneously, making it ideal for applications that require shared file access.

3. **High Availability and Durability**: EFS stores data redundantly across multiple availability zones (AZs) in the region, ensuring data is highly available and durable.

4. **Elastic Performance**: EFS provides consistent low latencies and high throughput, supporting a wide range of workloads from small applications to large-scale enterprise applications.

5. **Fully Managed**: AWS manages the underlying infrastructure, including patching, monitoring, and scaling, which reduces the operational burden on your team.

Benefits of Using EFS:

- **Ease of Use**: EFS is easy to set up and use with no complex configurations required. It integrates directly with EC2, Lambda, and other AWS services.
- **Cost Efficiency**: EFS offers a pay-as-you-go pricing model, meaning you only pay for the storage you use, with no upfront costs or long-term commitments.
- **Cross-platform Access**: EFS supports standard NFS protocols, allowing for compatibility with a wide range of applications, including legacy systems.
- **Seamless Integration with EC2**: EFS works directly with EC2 instances, making it ideal for cloud-native applications.

Setting Up EFS: How to Mount EFS on EC2 Instances

Creating an EFS File System To get started with Amazon EFS, you first need to create a file system in the AWS Management Console:

1. **Go to the EFS Console**:
   o Open the **Amazon EFS** section in the AWS Management Console.
2. **Create a New File System**:
   o Click **Create file system**.

- ○ Choose a **VPC** and **Availability Zones** for your file system. By default, EFS is available across multiple AZs in a region for high availability.
- ○ You can choose whether to enable **Encryption at Rest** (recommended for sensitive data) and configure other options, such as performance modes and throughput settings.

3. **Configure Network Access**:
   - ○ Select **Security Groups** for controlling access to your EFS file system. By default, the file system is private and accessible only to instances in the same VPC.
   - ○ Specify which EC2 instances or services can access the file system by configuring security group rules to allow inbound traffic on **NFS (port 2049)**.

4. **Create Mount Targets**:
   - ○ A **mount target** is created automatically in each Availability Zone. It provides an IP address and DNS name that EC2 instances can use to mount the EFS file system.

5. **Review and Create**:
   - ○ Once you've reviewed all settings, click **Create** to provision the file system.

Mounting EFS on EC2 Instances Once the EFS file system is created, you need to mount it on your EC2 instances to begin using it for storage:

1. **Install NFS Client**:
   - On your EC2 instances, you will need to install the **NFS client** (Amazon Linux 2 and most Linux distributions come with NFS pre-installed). If not, use the following command:

   ```bash

   sudo yum install -y nfs-utils
   ```

2. **Mount EFS Using the File System's DNS Name**:
   - Use the mount target's DNS name (which was created when you set up the EFS file system) to mount the file system on your EC2 instance.
   - Example mount command:

   ```bash

   sudo mount -t nfs4 fs-xxxxxx.efs.us-west-2.amazonaws.com:/ /mnt/efs
   ```

   - Replace `fs-xxxxxx` with your EFS file system's DNS name, and `/mnt/efs` with the directory on the EC2 instance where you want to mount the file system.

3. **Configure Auto-mount (Optional)**:

   o To ensure the EFS file system is mounted automatically when the EC2 instance reboots, add the mount entry to the /etc/fstab file:

   bash

   ```
   fs-xxxxxx.efs.us-west-
   2.amazonaws.com:/    /mnt/efs    nfs4
   defaults,_netdev 0 0
   ```

Real-World Example: Using EFS for Shared Storage Across Multiple Instances in a Web App

Let's consider a **web application** that serves user-uploaded content (e.g., images, videos) and needs to store files in a shared location that can be accessed by multiple EC2 instances. We will use **EFS** to handle this shared storage across instances.

Scenario: A media-sharing app needs to allow users to upload and view images and videos. The app is deployed across multiple EC2 instances in an auto-scaling group to handle varying traffic.

1. **Create EFS File System**:

159

- o The development team creates an EFS file system and ensures that the file system is configured to be available in all Availability Zones where the EC2 instances will be launched.
- o EFS is configured with encryption at rest for security, and access control is managed via security groups.

2. **Mount EFS on EC2 Instances**:

- o The team configures the EC2 instances (deployed in an **Auto Scaling Group**) to mount the EFS file system at /mnt/efs during startup using the **User Data script**. This ensures that every instance has access to the shared storage when it is launched.

User Data Example:

bash

```
#!/bin/bash
sudo yum install -y nfs-utils
sudo mount -t nfs4 fs-xxxxxx.efs.us-west-
2.amazonaws.com:/ /mnt/efs
```

3. **Using EFS in the Web Application**:

- o The application's code is modified to upload images to the mounted directory /mnt/efs. This ensures that any image uploaded by a user can be accessed by all EC2 instances in the Auto Scaling Group, allowing users to view the images regardless of which instance is serving the request.

- o For example, when a user uploads an image, the backend saves it to `/mnt/efs/uploads/{image_name}`. When the user requests the image, any EC2 instance can serve it from EFS.

4. **Handling Traffic Spikes**:

- o As the app scales and traffic increases, more EC2 instances are launched by the **Auto Scaling Group**. Each new instance automatically mounts the EFS file system, ensuring that the storage remains shared across all instances and can handle the increased load.

5. **Fault Tolerance**:

- o EFS is designed for high availability and durability, so even if an EC2 instance or an entire Availability Zone goes down, the data stored in EFS remains accessible to other instances in the same VPC.

Benefits of Using EFS in this Example:

- **Shared Storage**: All EC2 instances in the Auto Scaling Group can access the same data, ensuring consistency and availability of user-uploaded content.

- **Scalability**: EFS automatically scales as the app grows, handling more storage as more images and videos are uploaded without manual intervention.

- **High Availability**: With data stored in EFS across multiple Availability Zones, the app benefits from fault tolerance and minimized risk of data loss.

- **Simplified Management**: EFS removes the need to manage complex file storage solutions, allowing developers to focus on building the app.

In this chapter, we've explored **Amazon EFS**, a scalable and fully managed file storage service designed for shared access across multiple EC2 instances. We've learned how to create an EFS file system, mount it on EC2 instances, and integrate it with a web application to provide shared storage. The real-world example of using EFS for media storage in a web app demonstrated how EFS can handle file sharing, scalability, and fault tolerance. In the next chapters, we will discuss advanced EFS features, including performance tuning and integration with other AWS services.

CHAPTER 17

MONITORING WITH AMAZON CLOUDWATCH

In this chapter, we will explore **Amazon CloudWatch**, a powerful monitoring service for AWS resources and applications. CloudWatch provides real-time monitoring, logging, and alerting capabilities that help you maintain the health, performance, and security of your AWS environment. We will cover how to use CloudWatch for monitoring your AWS infrastructure, creating alarms and dashboards, managing log data, and setting up proactive alerts to ensure optimal performance. Additionally, we will walk through a real-world example of using CloudWatch to monitor EC2 instance health and performance metrics.

Introduction to CloudWatch: Monitoring AWS Resources and Applications

What is Amazon CloudWatch? Amazon CloudWatch is a comprehensive monitoring and observability service that provides data and actionable insights for AWS resources and applications. It collects metrics, logs, and events from various AWS services, and enables you to monitor and visualize the performance and health of your resources in real-time.

Key Features of CloudWatch:

1. **Metrics**: CloudWatch collects metrics such as CPU utilization, disk I/O, and network traffic from AWS services like EC2, RDS, Lambda, and more. It allows you to track the performance of resources and gain visibility into their behavior.

2. **Alarms**: CloudWatch alarms allow you to set thresholds for specific metrics. If a metric exceeds the threshold, the alarm triggers a notification or an action.

3. **Logs**: CloudWatch Logs allows you to collect, store, and analyze log data from your AWS resources and applications. It is essential for troubleshooting and gaining deeper insights into system behavior.

4. **Events**: CloudWatch Events provide near real-time notifications based on system events, such as EC2 instance state changes, Auto Scaling activity, or security alerts.

5. **Dashboards**: CloudWatch Dashboards enable you to create customizable visualizations of your metrics and alarms, offering an at-a-glance view of your AWS environment's health.

Why Use CloudWatch?

- **Proactive Monitoring**: CloudWatch allows you to monitor your AWS resources in real-time and proactively manage them by setting up alerts and alarms.
- **Cost Efficiency**: CloudWatch helps you optimize your AWS usage by monitoring resource utilization and scaling accordingly, ensuring that you're not over-provisioning or underutilizing your infrastructure.
- **Centralized Logging**: CloudWatch allows you to aggregate logs from multiple services and applications, making it easier to analyze and troubleshoot issues.

Creating Alarms and Dashboards: Setting Up Alerts for Proactive Management

Creating Alarms with CloudWatch CloudWatch allows you to create alarms based on various metrics. These alarms can be set to notify you when a specific threshold is breached or automatically trigger actions (like scaling an Auto Scaling group or running a Lambda function).

Steps to Create a CloudWatch Alarm:

1. **Go to the CloudWatch Console**:
   o Open the **Amazon CloudWatch** dashboard in the AWS Management Console.
2. **Create an Alarm**:

- o Click **Create Alarm** and choose a metric to monitor. For example, you can monitor metrics such as EC2 instance CPU utilization, RDS storage usage, or Lambda invocation count.

3. **Set Alarm Conditions**:
   - o Define the threshold for the alarm. For example, if CPU utilization exceeds 80% for a certain period (e.g., 5 minutes), the alarm triggers.

4. **Configure Actions**:
   - o Choose an action for when the alarm is triggered. You can send a notification via **SNS (Simple Notification Service)** to alert an administrator or take automatic actions (e.g., stop, terminate, or reboot an EC2 instance).

5. **Review and Create**:
   - o After configuring the alarm, review the settings and click **Create Alarm**. You will now be notified when the metric exceeds the defined threshold.

Best Practices for Alarms:

- **Set Meaningful Thresholds**: Avoid setting thresholds too high or low, as this can lead to either false positives or missed notifications.
- **Use Multiple Metrics**: Combine several metrics to get a complete view of resource health (e.g., combine CPU

166

utilization with disk I/O and network traffic for EC2 instances).

- **Create Alarm Actions**: Automate recovery by using alarms to trigger AWS Auto Scaling, Lambda functions, or other automated responses.

Creating Dashboards with CloudWatch CloudWatch Dashboards provide a centralized view of all your metrics and alarms in one place. You can create custom dashboards for different environments or applications to quickly assess system performance and health.

Steps to Create a CloudWatch Dashboard:

1. **Go to the CloudWatch Dashboard** in the AWS Console.
2. **Create a New Dashboard**:
   - Click **Create Dashboard**, give it a name, and choose a layout.
3. **Add Widgets to the Dashboard**:
   - Add widgets to display specific metrics, alarms, and visualizations. You can add line charts, stacked area charts, numbers, and more to visualize data over time.
4. **Customize**:
   - Choose which metrics to display. You can select metrics from EC2 instances, RDS databases, Lambda functions, etc.

167

5. **Save and Share**:

- o After creating the dashboard, save it and share the dashboard URL with other team members to keep everyone informed.

Best Practices for Dashboards:

- **Use Dashboards for Critical Metrics**: Focus on displaying high-priority metrics such as resource utilization, service health, and alarms.
- **Customize for Specific Teams**: Create separate dashboards for operations, security, or development teams to monitor the data relevant to their roles.
- **Review Dashboards Regularly**: Dashboards provide an at-a-glance overview of your environment, so it's important to review them regularly to ensure everything is running smoothly.

Log Management: Storing and Analyzing Log Data

CloudWatch Logs allows you to collect and analyze log data from AWS services and applications. It helps you gain deep insights into your systems, applications, and security events.

Setting Up CloudWatch Logs

1. **Create a Log Group**:

- o Log groups are logical containers for your logs. You can organize logs by application, service, or environment.
- o From the **CloudWatch Logs Console**, create a new log group by clicking **Create Log Group**.

2. **Create Log Streams**:
- o Log streams are individual records within a log group. For example, an EC2 instance may produce multiple log streams for different applications.
- o When you configure a service (such as EC2 or Lambda) to send logs to CloudWatch, it will create log streams for each instance or application.

3. **Send Logs to CloudWatch**:
- o You can configure AWS services like EC2, RDS, and Lambda to send logs to CloudWatch automatically.
- o For EC2, use the **CloudWatch Logs agent** to send application logs to CloudWatch Logs.

Analyzing Log Data CloudWatch Logs provides several ways to analyze log data:

- • **Log Insights**: CloudWatch Logs Insights is a powerful query engine that allows you to run queries against your log data to find patterns, errors, or performance issues.

- **CloudWatch Logs Metrics**: You can extract key metrics from your logs and use them in CloudWatch to create alarms or visualizations.

Example Query in Logs Insights:

```sql
fields @timestamp, @message
| filter @message like /error/
| sort @timestamp desc
| limit 20
```

This query filters for log messages containing the word "error" and sorts them by timestamp in descending order, displaying the 20 most recent errors.

Best Practices for Log Management:

- **Enable Logs for Key Resources**: Ensure that critical resources like EC2 instances, Lambda functions, and RDS databases are configured to send logs to CloudWatch.
- **Set Log Retention Policies**: Define how long logs are retained based on your compliance and operational requirements. You can configure retention policies to automatically delete old logs after a set period.

- **Monitor and Analyze Logs Proactively**: Use **CloudWatch Logs Insights** to analyze logs and set up alerts for unusual patterns (e.g., error messages or high latency).

Real-World Example: Monitoring EC2 Instance Health and Performance Metrics

Let's consider a scenario where you need to monitor the **health and performance** of EC2 instances running a web application. Monitoring these instances ensures that the application is available and responsive.

Step 1: Collect Key Metrics

- **CPU Utilization**: Track CPU usage to detect performance bottlenecks or over-provisioned instances.
- **Disk I/O**: Monitor disk read/write operations to ensure that storage performance is sufficient for the workload.
- **Network Traffic**: Track incoming and outgoing network traffic to detect slow or blocked network connections.

Step 2: Create CloudWatch Alarms

- **CPU Utilization Alarm**: Set an alarm to trigger if CPU utilization exceeds 80% for more than 5 minutes, indicating that the instance is under heavy load.

o   Action: Send an SNS notification to the system administrator to investigate and potentially scale the EC2 instance.

- **Disk I/O Alarm**: Set an alarm if disk read/write operations exceed a certain threshold, which could indicate that the instance is underperforming.

  o   Action: Trigger an Auto Scaling action to launch a new instance if the disk I/O performance is below the required threshold for more than 10 minutes.

Step 3: Create CloudWatch Dashboards

- Create a **CloudWatch Dashboard** to visualize key EC2 instance metrics, such as CPU utilization, network traffic, and disk I/O, for quick monitoring of the application's health.

- This dashboard can be accessed by the operations team for real-time monitoring of instance performance.

Step 4: Analyze Logs

- Set up **CloudWatch Logs** to capture application logs from the EC2 instances. Use **CloudWatch Logs Insights** to query the logs for errors or slow request responses, helping the team identify any issues with the application.

Step 5: Set Up Auto Scaling

- Configure **Auto Scaling** based on CloudWatch alarms, automatically adding or removing EC2 instances depending on the health and performance metrics. This ensures that your application remains responsive even during traffic spikes.

In this chapter, we've explored **Amazon CloudWatch**, a powerful service for monitoring AWS resources and applications. We covered how to create alarms and dashboards to track metrics, how to manage and analyze log data, and how to use CloudWatch to monitor EC2 instance health and performance. CloudWatch provides proactive monitoring, helping you ensure the optimal performance of your infrastructure and applications. In the next chapters, we will explore more advanced CloudWatch features, such as custom metrics, CloudWatch Logs Insights, and integration with other AWS services.

CHAPTER 18

AWS COST MANAGEMENT AND OPTIMIZATION

In this chapter, we will explore **AWS Cost Management and Optimization** tools and best practices. Understanding how AWS pricing works and how to track, control, and optimize costs is critical for running efficient, cost-effective applications. We will discuss the different pricing models, how to use tools like **Cost Explorer** and **Budgets**, and strategies for optimizing costs. Finally, we'll walk through a real-world example of optimizing costs for a startup running a production web application.

Understanding AWS Pricing Models: Pay-as-You-Go, Reserved Instances, Spot Instances

AWS Pricing Models AWS offers various pricing models that give you flexibility in how you pay for services. Understanding these models helps you choose the most cost-effective approach based on your usage patterns.

1. **Pay-as-You-Go (On-Demand)**:
    o In the **Pay-as-you-Go** model, you pay for AWS services on a per-hour or per-second basis

174

(depending on the service). There are no upfront costs or long-term commitments, and you can scale your resources up or down as needed.

- o **Use Case**: Ideal for applications with unpredictable or variable workloads, where you need flexibility and the ability to quickly scale resources based on demand.
- o **Example**: Running a small application or dev/test environment where you only need resources occasionally.

2. **Reserved Instances (RIs)**:

- o With **Reserved Instances**, you commit to using a specific AWS resource (e.g., EC2 instances, RDS databases) for a one- or three-year term. In exchange for this commitment, you receive a significant discount (up to 75%) compared to on-demand pricing.
- o **Use Case**: Suitable for applications with steady, predictable workloads that require long-term capacity.
- o **Types of Reserved Instances**:
    - **Standard RIs**: Provide the largest discounts but offer less flexibility for instance changes.
    - **Convertible RIs**: Offer flexibility to change instance types during the

reservation term, though at a slightly lower discount.

- o **Example**: Running a production environment that needs consistent EC2 capacity for the next 1-3 years.

3. **Spot Instances**:

- o **Spot Instances** allow you to bid for unused AWS capacity at a significantly reduced price (up to 90% off on-demand pricing). However, Spot Instances can be interrupted by AWS with little notice if the demand for capacity increases.
- o **Use Case**: Ideal for workloads that are flexible and can tolerate interruptions, such as batch processing, big data analytics, or testing.
- o **Example**: Running non-critical jobs like data processing or machine learning model training where interruptions are acceptable.

Key Pricing Considerations:

- **Use Reserved Instances for Predictable Workloads**: If you have steady, predictable workloads, Reserved Instances can provide significant savings.
- **Use Spot Instances for Non-Critical Workloads**: If you have flexible workloads, Spot Instances can offer substantial savings with the potential for interruption.

- **On-Demand for Flexibility**: If your workload is unpredictable or short-term, the Pay-as-you-Go model is the most flexible but comes at a higher cost.

Cost Explorer and Budgets: Tracking and Controlling Costs

AWS Cost Explorer: **Cost Explorer** is a tool that allows you to visualize, analyze, and track AWS costs and usage over time. It provides detailed insights into your spending, helping you identify trends and areas where you can optimize costs.

Key Features of Cost Explorer:

1. **Usage Reports**: View your usage data for different AWS services, such as EC2, S3, RDS, and more.
2. **Cost Forecasting**: Predict future costs based on historical usage data, helping you plan your budget and allocate resources efficiently.
3. **Cost Allocation Tags**: Use cost allocation tags to group and categorize your AWS resources, allowing you to see costs for specific projects, teams, or departments.
4. **Service Comparison**: Compare usage and costs across different AWS services, identifying areas where you can consolidate or switch to lower-cost options.

5. **Custom Reports**: Create custom reports to analyze spending patterns and breakdowns by regions, services, or linked accounts.

Using Cost Explorer for Cost Optimization:

- **Identify High-Cost Services**: By regularly reviewing your usage data in Cost Explorer, you can identify which services are consuming the most resources and consider optimizing them (e.g., rightsizing EC2 instances or switching to cheaper storage options).
- **Spot Instance Usage**: Use Cost Explorer to track Spot Instance usage and see how much you're saving compared to on-demand instances.

AWS Budgets: **AWS Budgets** allows you to set custom cost and usage budgets and track your progress towards those budgets. You can set up notifications to alert you when your spending exceeds a defined threshold.

Key Features of AWS Budgets:

1. **Cost Budgets**: Set a monthly or annual cost limit for your AWS usage. If your spending exceeds this budget, AWS will send you an email notification.
2. **Usage Budgets**: Track usage of specific AWS resources (e.g., EC2 instances, S3 storage) and set usage limits to

ensure you don't exceed your expected resource consumption.

3. **Reservation Budgets**: Track Reserved Instance utilization and ensure that you're making the most of your reserved capacity.

Using AWS Budgets for Cost Management:

- **Set Alerts**: You can set thresholds for when your spending or usage exceeds a certain limit, ensuring that you stay on top of your AWS costs.

- **Track Savings Plans and Reserved Instances**: Use AWS Budgets to monitor your Reserved Instances and Savings Plans utilization to ensure you're getting the full benefit of these cost-saving options.

Cost Optimization Best Practices: Rightsizing Instances, Choosing Cheaper Services

Rightsizing Instances:

- **Rightsizing** involves selecting the most appropriate instance size based on your actual workload requirements. By ensuring that your EC2 instances are not over-provisioned, you can significantly reduce costs.

  o Use **AWS Compute Optimizer** to get recommendations on how to rightsize EC2 instances based on past usage patterns.

  o Review **CloudWatch metrics** to monitor CPU, memory, and disk usage to ensure your instances are not underutilized.

Choosing Cheaper Services:

- **Switch to Cheaper Instance Types**: If you are using larger EC2 instance types than necessary, consider switching to smaller or more cost-effective instance types (e.g., from `m5.large` to `t3.micro`).

- **Use Spot and Reserved Instances**: Leverage **Spot Instances** for non-critical workloads that can tolerate interruptions and **Reserved Instances** for steady, predictable workloads.

- **Use S3 Storage Classes**: For data that isn't frequently accessed, use cheaper S3 storage classes like **S3 Glacier** or **S3 One Zone-IA** to reduce costs.

- **Leverage Savings Plans**: AWS **Savings Plans** offer flexible pricing models for EC2 and Fargate workloads, allowing you to save up to 72% on long-term usage.

- **Use Serverless Options**: Where possible, use **serverless** services like **AWS Lambda** instead of EC2 instances. Serverless computing charges only for the execution time, saving costs when workloads are variable or sporadic.

Monitor and Analyze Costs Regularly:

- Set up a monthly review of your **Cost Explorer** and **AWS Budgets** to assess your usage and adjust resources based on your findings. Regular monitoring can help you spot inefficiencies early and optimize your spending before it becomes an issue.

Real-World Example: Optimizing Costs for a Startup Running a Production Web App

Let's consider a **startup running a production web app** that wants to optimize AWS costs while maintaining performance and scalability.

Scenario: The startup is running a web application on AWS using EC2 instances, RDS databases, and S3 for storage. As traffic increases, they notice that their AWS costs are rising faster than expected.

Step 1: Analyze Current Usage with Cost Explorer

- The startup uses **AWS Cost Explorer** to identify the top services contributing to their costs. They find that EC2 instances are consuming a significant portion of their budget, particularly for small instances that are underutilized.

- They also notice that their S3 storage costs are high due to using the **S3 Standard** class for all data, including infrequently accessed files.

Step 2: Rightsize EC2 Instances

- The startup uses **AWS Compute Optimizer** and **CloudWatch** metrics to determine that many of their EC2 instances are over-provisioned.
- They downgrade from **m5.large** instances to **t3.medium** instances for most of their web application servers, reducing costs by 40% while still maintaining performance.
- They also switch several non-critical instances to **Spot Instances**, saving another 60%.

Step 3: Move Infrequent Data to Cheaper Storage

- The startup moves older user data and logs that are infrequently accessed to **S3 Glacier** and **S3 One Zone-IA**, reducing S3 storage costs by 30%.

Step 4: Leverage Savings Plans

- The startup evaluates their EC2 usage and purchases an **EC2 Savings Plan** for their steady-state usage, saving up to 72% compared to on-demand pricing.

Step 5: Set Up AWS Budgets

- The startup sets up an **AWS Budget** to track monthly spending on EC2, RDS, and S3 services, with alerts set to notify them when they approach their target budget.

Step 6: Ongoing Cost Monitoring

- The startup sets a monthly review schedule to track cost changes, ensuring they continue to optimize their resources based on the evolving needs of their web application.

Results:

- By rightsizing instances, moving infrequent data to cheaper storage, and leveraging Savings Plans, the startup reduces its AWS costs by 35%, while maintaining performance and scalability for their web application.

In this chapter, we've discussed **AWS Cost Management and Optimization** strategies, including understanding AWS pricing models, using **Cost Explorer** and **AWS Budgets** for tracking costs, and implementing best practices for cost optimization. The real-world example showed how a startup can optimize costs while scaling a production web app. By monitoring and analyzing usage regularly, and making adjustments based on that data, businesses can reduce their AWS costs significantly while maintaining efficient and performant cloud infrastructure. In the next chapters, we will explore more advanced cost optimization strategies, including the use of **AWS Trusted Advisor** and **AWS Cost and Usage Reports** for more granular insights.

CHAPTER 19

AWS SECURITY BEST PRACTICES

In this chapter, we will explore the best practices for securing your AWS environment, from understanding the **AWS Shared Responsibility Model** to implementing encryption for data protection and conducting vulnerability scanning for compliance. Security is a critical aspect of managing AWS resources, and knowing how to secure your infrastructure will help you mitigate risks and protect your data. We will also go through a real-world example of securing an **eCommerce app** using SSL/TLS for secure communication and encrypting data with AWS **Key Management Service (KMS)**.

AWS Shared Responsibility Model: Understanding What AWS Secures vs. What You Secure

What is the Shared Responsibility Model? The **Shared Responsibility Model** defines the security responsibilities of both AWS and its customers. AWS takes responsibility for the **security of the cloud**, meaning the physical infrastructure, hardware, and the software that runs the AWS services. Customers, on the other

185

hand, are responsible for the **security in the cloud**, which includes securing the resources and data they deploy within AWS.

AWS Responsibilities (Security *of* the Cloud):

- **Physical Security**: AWS manages the security of its data centers, including physical access controls and environmental safeguards (e.g., fire suppression, power redundancy).
- **Networking**: AWS provides secure networking capabilities such as **Virtual Private Cloud (VPC)**, **firewalls**, and **load balancing**.
- **Compute**: AWS manages the underlying infrastructure of compute services like **EC2** instances, **Lambda functions**, and **Fargate**.
- **Storage**: AWS secures the underlying storage infrastructure, such as **EBS (Elastic Block Store)**, **S3**, and **Glacier**.

Customer Responsibilities (Security *in* the Cloud):

- **Data Protection**: Customers are responsible for securing their data, including **encryption**, **backup**, and **data access control**.
- **Access Control**: Customers manage **Identity and Access Management (IAM)** roles and policies to ensure that only authorized users can access their resources.

- **Network Configuration**: Customers configure **VPC**, **security groups**, and **NACLs (Network Access Control Lists)** to control traffic between instances and services.

- **Application Security**: Customers ensure that their applications, including those running on EC2 instances or Lambda, are secure and free from vulnerabilities.

By understanding the Shared Responsibility Model, you can ensure that your AWS environment is secured in line with best practices and compliance requirements.

Encryption at Rest and in Transit: Securing Data Using KMS (Key Management Service)

What is Encryption at Rest and in Transit?

- **Encryption at Rest**: This refers to encrypting data while it is stored, either on physical disks, in databases, or in cloud storage services like **Amazon S3**. Encrypting data at rest ensures that it is protected even if the storage device is compromised.

- **Encryption in Transit**: This refers to encrypting data while it is being transmitted over networks, ensuring that it cannot be intercepted or altered during transmission. Common protocols for encryption in transit include **SSL/TLS** and **IPsec**.

Why is Encryption Important?

- **Data Protection**: Encryption prevents unauthorized access to sensitive data, whether it's at rest or in transit.
- **Compliance**: Many industries (e.g., healthcare, finance) require data encryption to meet regulatory compliance standards (e.g., **HIPAA, PCI-DSS**).
- **Security Breach Mitigation**: Even if data is stolen, encrypted data is useless without the encryption keys.

Using AWS Key Management Service (KMS) AWS KMS is a fully managed service that allows you to create and control the encryption keys used to encrypt your data. KMS integrates seamlessly with other AWS services and provides a centralized way to manage encryption.

Key Features of KMS:

1. **Customer-Managed Keys**: You can create, manage, and control access to your own encryption keys.
2. **AWS Managed Keys**: For some services (e.g., S3, EBS), AWS provides default managed keys to simplify encryption setup.
3. **Key Policies**: Define who can use and manage keys using IAM policies and key policies.

4. **Audit and Monitoring**: KMS integrates with **AWS CloudTrail**, allowing you to monitor and log key usage and access.

Encrypting Data with KMS:

- **For Data at Rest**: Enable encryption for S3 buckets, RDS databases, or EBS volumes. When you create or modify a resource, select the appropriate KMS key to encrypt the data.
- **For Data in Transit**: Use **SSL/TLS** certificates for secure communication between services and clients. KMS can be used to manage SSL/TLS certificates with **AWS Certificate Manager (ACM)**.

Best Practices for Encryption:

- **Enable encryption by default** for all new data stored in services like S3, RDS, and EBS.
- **Use IAM policies** to control who has access to encryption keys.
- **Rotate keys regularly** using KMS key rotation features to ensure maximum security.

Vulnerability Scanning and Compliance: Securing Your Cloud Infrastructure

Vulnerability Scanning Vulnerability scanning is the process of identifying weaknesses in your infrastructure or application that could be exploited by an attacker. Regular scanning helps identify security risks before they can be exploited.

AWS Tools for Vulnerability Scanning:

1. **Amazon Inspector**: A security assessment service that automatically scans your EC2 instances for vulnerabilities and deviations from best practices. It provides detailed findings and recommendations for remediation.

2. **AWS Security Hub**: A centralized security service that aggregates findings from Amazon Inspector, AWS GuardDuty, and other AWS services. It provides a comprehensive view of your security posture.

3. **AWS Trusted Advisor**: Offers security checks for best practices in areas such as IAM, encryption, and security group configurations.

Compliance and Governance AWS provides various tools to help you meet industry standards and regulatory requirements:

1. **AWS Config**: Tracks configuration changes in your AWS resources and helps you maintain compliance with internal and external policies.

190

2. **AWS Audit Manager**: Automates the collection of evidence needed for audits and helps you maintain continuous compliance with standards like **SOC 2, ISO 27001**, and **GDPR**.

3. **AWS Artifact**: Provides on-demand access to AWS's compliance reports, certifications, and security documentation.

Best Practices for Security and Compliance:

- **Regularly scan for vulnerabilities** using Amazon Inspector and other scanning tools.

- **Review and audit access controls** for AWS resources to ensure that only authorized users have access.

- **Monitor and respond to security events** using **AWS GuardDuty**, which helps detect malicious activity and abnormal behavior in your AWS account.

- **Maintain compliance** with industry standards by using AWS services like **AWS Config** and **Audit Manager** to track and report compliance status.

Real-World Example: Securing an eCommerce App with SSL/TLS and Data Encryption

Let's consider a **startup running an eCommerce web application**. The app handles sensitive customer information such as payment details, shipping addresses, and order history. The team needs to ensure that the application is secure and complies with industry standards for data protection.

Step 1: Enabling SSL/TLS for Secure Communication

- The team configures **SSL/TLS** certificates to encrypt data in transit between customers' browsers and the application server. This ensures that sensitive data such as credit card numbers is encrypted during transmission.
- **AWS Certificate Manager (ACM)** is used to provision and manage the SSL certificates, simplifying the management of encryption keys and certificates for secure connections.

Step 2: Encrypting Data at Rest

- The eCommerce platform stores customer data (e.g., payment information, order details) in an **RDS instance**. To secure this data, the team enables **encryption at rest** using AWS **KMS**. This ensures that data in the RDS database is encrypted and protected from unauthorized access, even if the database or storage is compromised.
- **S3** is used for storing user-uploaded images, and encryption is enabled for the S3 bucket using a KMS-managed key to ensure all media files are encrypted at rest.

Step 3: Regular Vulnerability Scanning

- The team regularly runs **Amazon Inspector** on EC2 instances hosting the web application to identify vulnerabilities in the server configuration and application code.
- Findings from the vulnerability scans are reviewed, and necessary patches are applied to address any identified security weaknesses.

Step 4: Monitoring and Compliance

- The team sets up **AWS CloudTrail** to log and monitor API calls to the AWS infrastructure. This allows them to track who is accessing and modifying resources in the AWS account.
- **AWS Config** is used to monitor the configuration of AWS resources, ensuring that security best practices are adhered to and that any misconfigurations are flagged for remediation.

Benefits of Securing the eCommerce App:

- **Secure User Data**: By encrypting data both in transit and at rest, the team ensures that customer data is protected from eavesdropping, tampering, and unauthorized access.
- **Compliance**: Using SSL/TLS, encryption, and regular vulnerability scanning helps the team meet industry

compliance requirements such as **PCI-DSS** for handling payment information.

- **Proactive Monitoring**: By using tools like **CloudTrail** and **AWS Config**, the team can quickly detect and respond to any security incidents or misconfigurations, reducing the risk of a security breach.

In this chapter, we've covered **AWS security best practices**, including the **Shared Responsibility Model**, data encryption with **KMS**, and vulnerability scanning with tools like **Amazon Inspector**. We also demonstrated how to secure an **eCommerce app** using SSL/TLS for encrypted communication and data encryption for sensitive storage. By following these security best practices and leveraging AWS tools, you can ensure the confidentiality, integrity, and availability of your cloud infrastructure. In the next chapters, we will explore more advanced security features, including **AWS WAF**, **AWS Shield**, and **IAM best practices** for securing access to AWS resources.

CHAPTER 20

AWS BACKUP AND DISASTER RECOVERY

In this chapter, we will delve into **AWS Backup** and **Disaster Recovery** strategies, which are essential for ensuring the continuity and availability of your applications and data. AWS provides powerful services for backing up and recovering your infrastructure, helping you mitigate the risks of data loss and service downtime. We will explore how to set up backup strategies using AWS tools like **AWS Backup**, **snapshots**, and **Amazon Machine Images (AMIs)**. Additionally, we will discuss disaster recovery planning, including defining key metrics like **Recovery Time Objective (RTO)** and **Recovery Point Objective (RPO)**. Finally, we will walk through a real-world example of setting up a disaster recovery plan for a **media company's archives**.

Backup Strategies: Using AWS Backup, Snapshots, and AMIs

What is AWS Backup? AWS Backup is a fully managed service that automates backup processes for various AWS services, including EC2, EBS, RDS, DynamoDB, and more. It allows you to centrally manage backup schedules, retention policies, and compliance, ensuring that your data is protected and can be restored when needed.

AWS Backup Key Features:

1. **Centralized Backup Management**: AWS Backup provides a single console to manage backups across AWS services, making it easier to ensure consistency and compliance.
2. **Automated Backups**: You can automate backup schedules for various resources, such as databases, file systems, and EC2 instances, reducing the risk of human error.
3. **Retention Policies**: AWS Backup allows you to define how long backups should be retained and automatically deletes expired backups to reduce storage costs.
4. **Cross-Region Backups**: AWS Backup enables you to replicate backups across AWS regions for disaster recovery purposes.

Using Snapshots and AMIs for Backup:

- **EBS Snapshots**: AWS allows you to create **snapshots** of **Elastic Block Store (EBS)** volumes. Snapshots are incremental, meaning that only the data that has changed since the last snapshot is backed up, making them efficient in terms of storage.

o **Use Case**: Snapshots are useful for creating point-in-time backups of data stored on EBS volumes. You can restore an EBS volume from a snapshot if the data is lost or corrupted.

- **Amazon Machine Images (AMIs)**: **AMIs** are backups of EC2 instances, including the instance configuration, operating system, and application data. AMIs provide a way to quickly recreate an EC2 instance from an image.

  o **Use Case**: AMIs are ideal for backing up complete EC2 instance configurations, allowing you to recreate the instance and its environment in the event of a failure.

Best Practices for Backups:

- **Automate Backups**: Use AWS Backup to automate backups for critical AWS resources like EC2, RDS, and DynamoDB, ensuring that backups are created consistently and without manual intervention.

- **Backup Frequency**: Set appropriate backup intervals (e.g., daily, weekly) based on your business needs. Frequent backups may be necessary for highly dynamic workloads, while less frequent backups may suffice for more static data.

- **Test Restores**: Periodically test the restoration process to ensure that your backups are valid and that you can recover data quickly when needed.

- **Use Cross-Region Backups**: Replicate backups to another region for disaster recovery to ensure business continuity in case of regional outages.

Disaster Recovery Planning: Recovery Time Objectives (RTO) and Recovery Point Objectives (RPO)

What is Disaster Recovery (DR)? Disaster Recovery refers to the process of restoring systems and data after a catastrophic event, such as hardware failure, natural disaster, cyberattack, or service outage. A comprehensive DR plan ensures that your organization can resume operations quickly, minimizing downtime and data loss.

Key Metrics in Disaster Recovery Planning:

1. **Recovery Time Objective (RTO)**:
   o **Definition**: RTO is the maximum allowable downtime for an application or service. It defines the target time within which a system or application must be restored after a failure.
   o **Example**: If an application has an RTO of 4 hours, it means that in the event of a failure, the system must be restored and fully functional within 4 hours to meet business requirements.

2. **Recovery Point Objective (RPO)**:

- o **Definition**: RPO is the maximum acceptable amount of data loss in the event of a failure. It defines how frequently backups should be taken to ensure that data loss is minimized.
- o **Example**: If the RPO is 1 hour, it means that in the event of a failure, you can accept losing up to 1 hour's worth of data, and backups should be taken at least every hour to meet this objective.

AWS Disaster Recovery Solutions:

1. **Backup and Restore**: This is the simplest form of disaster recovery, where data and application configurations are regularly backed up, and in the event of a failure, the system is restored from those backups.
   - o **Use Case**: Suitable for systems with a higher RPO, where data loss is acceptable, and recovery time is longer.

2. **Pilot Light**: In this approach, a minimal version of the application is always running in the cloud, and in the event of a failure, additional resources are quickly provisioned to scale up the application.
   - o **Use Case**: Suitable for systems with a lower RTO but where some downtime is acceptable.

3. **Warm Standby**: A scaled-down version of the application is running continuously, and in the event of a failure, it can be scaled up quickly to full capacity.

199

o **Use Case**: Suitable for systems with low RTO and medium RPO, where quick recovery is important but the full system doesn't need to be running at all times.

4. **Multi-Site Active-Active**: In this approach, the application runs in multiple regions or availability zones simultaneously. If one region goes down, the other regions continue to handle the traffic, ensuring no downtime.

o **Use Case**: Ideal for critical applications that need near-zero downtime and a low RPO.

Choosing the Right DR Strategy:

- Assess your **RTO** and **RPO** requirements for each application. For example, critical applications may require a **warm standby** or **multi-site active-active** approach, while less critical applications can use **backup and restore**.

Real-World Example: Setting Up Disaster Recovery for a Media Company's Archives

Let's consider a **media company** that stores vast amounts of video and image files in AWS. These files are critical for the company's business, and they need to ensure that they can quickly recover data in case of a disaster, such as a data center failure or a cyberattack.

Step 1: Understand RTO and RPO

- The media company sets an **RTO** of **4 hours** and an **RPO** of **1 hour**. This means that if the system goes down, they must be able to restore the application within 4 hours, and they can afford to lose up to 1 hour of data.

Step 2: Set Up Backups

- The company uses **AWS Backup** to create regular backups of their media files stored in **S3** and their **EC2 instances** running media processing applications.
- The media company ensures that backups are taken every hour to meet the 1-hour RPO, and stores backups in **multiple regions** for disaster recovery.

Step 3: Choose a Disaster Recovery Strategy

- The media company adopts a **warm standby** approach, where a scaled-down version of the media processing application is always running in a secondary AWS region. In the event of a primary region failure, the system can be scaled up within a few hours to meet the 4-hour RTO.

Step 4: Set Up Multi-Region S3 Replication

- The media company enables **Cross-Region Replication (CRR)** for their **S3 buckets** to ensure that media files are replicated across regions in real-time. This reduces data loss risk and ensures that media files are always available in case of a region failure.

Step 5: Monitoring and Testing

- The company uses **AWS CloudWatch** to monitor the health of the backup process and to ensure that backups are completed successfully.
- Regularly scheduled **disaster recovery drills** are conducted to test the recovery process, ensuring that they can meet the RTO and RPO.

Step 6: Automate Recovery

- The company automates the recovery process using **AWS CloudFormation** templates to quickly spin up resources and restore the application's infrastructure, including EC2 instances, storage, and networking configurations.

Results:

- The media company now has a disaster recovery plan in place that meets its RTO and RPO requirements. In the event of a disaster, they can restore their application within 4 hours, with minimal data loss, ensuring business continuity.

In this chapter, we've covered **AWS Backup and Disaster Recovery** strategies, including understanding the **AWS Shared Responsibility Model** for security, backup strategies using AWS services like **AWS Backup**, **snapshots**, and **AMIs**, and planning for disaster recovery with **RTO** and **RPO**. We also explored a real-world example of setting up disaster recovery for a media company's archives. By following these best practices, you can ensure that your AWS environment is resilient, secure, and ready to recover in case of unexpected failures. In the next chapters, we will dive deeper into specific disaster recovery techniques and automation tools available in AWS.

CHAPTER 21

AWS FOR MOBILE APP DEVELOPMENT

In this chapter, we will explore how **AWS** can be leveraged to build, deploy, and scale **mobile applications**. AWS offers a suite of services designed specifically for mobile app developers, including **AWS Amplify** for rapid mobile app development, **Amazon Cognito** for secure user authentication, and other tools to create a fully-featured backend for your mobile app. We will also walk through a real-world example of developing and deploying a mobile app with an AWS backend.

Using AWS Amplify: Building and Deploying Mobile Apps with AWS

What is AWS Amplify? AWS Amplify is a set of tools and services that enables mobile and web app developers to build scalable and secure applications on AWS. Amplify simplifies the process of integrating AWS services like **Cognito, API Gateway, S3, Lambda**, and others into your mobile app, allowing you to focus on writing app code rather than managing infrastructure.

Key Features of AWS Amplify:

1. **Backend Development**: Amplify provides a simple way to set up and manage backend services such as databases, user authentication, and storage, without having to write extensive server-side code.

2. **Authentication and Authorization**: Amplify integrates with **Cognito** to provide secure user authentication, including support for social logins (e.g., Google, Facebook) and multi-factor authentication (MFA).

3. **Hosting**: Amplify provides a fully managed hosting service that allows you to deploy and host static web and mobile apps with automatic scaling.

4. **Data Storage**: Amplify allows you to connect to AWS services like **DynamoDB** for NoSQL storage and **S3** for file storage, making it easy to manage data for your mobile apps.

5. **Push Notifications**: Amplify integrates with **Amazon Pinpoint** to send push notifications, emails, and SMS messages to users.

6. **Analytics**: Amplify provides built-in analytics to track user behavior and engagement with your app.

Setting Up AWS Amplify for Mobile Development:

1. **Install the Amplify CLI**: Start by installing the Amplify Command Line Interface (CLI) on your local machine. The CLI helps you create and manage backend resources in your AWS account.

```
bash
```

```
npm install -g @aws-amplify/cli
amplify configure
```

The `amplify configure` command sets up the AWS credentials to use Amplify.

2. **Initialize a New Project**: In your mobile app project, run:

```
bash
```

```
amplify init
```

This will create a new Amplify project and configure it with your AWS account.

3. **Add Backend Services**: You can easily add backend services such as authentication, APIs, and databases:
   - **Authentication**: Use Amplify to add **Cognito** authentication with:

     ```
     bash
     ```

     ```
     amplify add auth
     ```

   - **API**: Set up a REST or GraphQL API with:

     ```
     bash
     ```

```
amplify add api
```

o **Storage**: Add file storage (e.g., for user-uploaded images) with:

```
bash
```

```
amplify add storage
```

4. **Deploy the Backend**: Once your backend services are set up, deploy them to AWS with the following command:

```
bash
```

```
amplify push
```

This will provision the necessary AWS resources (e.g., Cognito, DynamoDB, Lambda) and set up the connections to your mobile app.

5. **Integrate Amplify with Your Mobile App**: To integrate Amplify with your mobile app, you need to install the **AWS Amplify SDK** in your app:

```
bash
```

```
npm install aws-amplify
```

After installing, configure Amplify in your mobile app by adding the configuration code:

207

```javascript

import Amplify from 'aws-amplify';
import awsconfig from './aws-exports';

Amplify.configure(awsconfig);
```

The `aws-exports` file is automatically created when you run `amplify push`, and it contains all the necessary configuration to connect your app to the AWS backend.

Cognito for User Authentication: Secure Login and User Management

What is Amazon Cognito? Amazon Cognito is a fully managed service that handles user authentication, authorization, and user data management for your mobile and web applications. With Cognito, you can easily add sign-up, sign-in, and access control features to your apps, supporting social logins (like Facebook or Google), enterprise logins via SAML, and multi-factor authentication (MFA) for added security.

Key Features of Amazon Cognito:

1. **User Pools**: A **User Pool** is a user directory that helps you manage user registration, authentication, and account

208

recovery. It's ideal for handling sign-ups and sign-ins for mobile apps.

2. **Identity Pools**: **Identity Pools** allow you to grant authenticated users access to AWS services such as S3, DynamoDB, and more. This feature enables fine-grained access control.

3. **Federated Identities**: Cognito supports **federated identities**, meaning you can allow users to log in via social identity providers like **Google**, **Facebook**, or **Amazon**, or through **SAML-based** corporate identity systems.

4. **Multi-Factor Authentication (MFA)**: Cognito supports MFA to enhance security by requiring users to verify their identity with a second factor, such as a one-time password (OTP) sent to their phone.

Setting Up Cognito Authentication with AWS Amplify:

1. **Add Authentication to Your Amplify Project**: From your project directory, run:

```bash

amplify add auth
```

This will allow you to configure user authentication for your mobile app. Amplify makes it easy to choose from default authentication settings or customize it with more advanced features like MFA and social logins.

2. **Configure the User Pool**: During setup, you can configure **User Pools** with settings such as password strength, email verification, and MFA. You can also define custom authentication flows for more complex use cases.

3. **Deploy and Sync**: After configuring Cognito, run:

```bash
amplify push
```

This deploys the authentication settings to your AWS environment and updates the `aws-exports` file in your mobile app.

4. **Integrate Cognito into Your Mobile App**: In your mobile app, you can now use the Amplify library to authenticate users. For example, to sign in a user:

```javascript
import { Auth } from 'aws-amplify';

async function signIn(username, password)
{
    try {
```

```
    const          user          =          await
Auth.signIn(username, password);
    console.log(user);
  } catch (error) {
    console.error("Error   signing   in",
error);
  }
}
```

Real-World Example: Developing and Deploying a Mobile App with AWS Backend

Scenario: A **startup company** is developing a mobile app to allow users to view and upload product images. The app requires secure user authentication, a backend API to manage product data, and storage for user-uploaded images.

Step 1: Set Up AWS Amplify:

- The team initializes an Amplify project using `amplify init` and then adds **authentication** with `amplify add auth` to enable user sign-up, sign-in, and password recovery.
- They also add an **API** using `amplify add api` to handle product data, and **storage** using `amplify add storage` for managing image uploads.

211

Step 2: Configure Cognito Authentication:

- Using **Cognito**, the team configures a **User Pool** to handle user registration, login, and MFA. They enable social login via **Google** for easy sign-up and sign-in options.

Step 3: Deploy Backend:

- The team deploys the backend resources with `amplify push`, which sets up the Cognito User Pool, API Gateway, Lambda functions, and S3 buckets for image storage.

Step 4: Connect Mobile App to AWS:

- In the mobile app, the team installs the Amplify SDK and configures the app to use the Cognito User Pool for authentication and the API Gateway for managing product data.
- They implement authentication screens (login, sign-up) and use Amplify to sign in users, upload images to S3, and retrieve product data through the API.

Step 5: Testing and Deployment:

- After developing the app and connecting it to the AWS backend, the team tests it to ensure users can sign in securely, upload images, and retrieve product data.

- The app is deployed to the **App Store** (for iOS) and **Google Play** (for Android), and the backend scales automatically with **AWS Lambda** and **API Gateway**.

In this chapter, we've explored how to use **AWS Amplify** to rapidly build and deploy mobile applications, how to integrate **Amazon Cognito** for user authentication, and how to connect your mobile app to an AWS backend for managing data and storage. The real-world example illustrated how these tools can be used together to develop a fully-featured mobile app with secure user authentication, an API, and scalable storage. By leveraging AWS, mobile developers can focus on building great user experiences without worrying about backend infrastructure. In the next chapters, we will dive deeper into additional mobile app services such as **AWS AppSync** for GraphQL APIs and **Amazon Pinpoint** for targeted user messaging and analytics.

CHAPTER 22

AWS FOR MACHINE LEARNING

In this chapter, we will explore the powerful machine learning (ML) capabilities provided by AWS through a variety of services such as **Amazon SageMaker, Amazon Rekognition, Amazon Polly**, and **Amazon Lex**. AWS offers a broad suite of managed services that allow developers and data scientists to build, train, and deploy machine learning models with ease. We will also go through a real-world example of using **AWS Rekognition** for facial recognition in security applications, demonstrating how these tools can be integrated into real-world scenarios.

AWS Machine Learning Services: SageMaker, Rekognition, Polly, Lex

AWS provides several fully managed services that cater to different aspects of machine learning, from building models to integrating AI-driven capabilities into applications.

1. Amazon SageMaker: Building and Training ML Models
Amazon SageMaker is a comprehensive, fully managed service that provides every tool you need to build, train, and deploy machine learning models at scale. SageMaker eliminates the

heavy lifting of setting up and managing the infrastructure required for ML model development.

Key Features of Amazon SageMaker:

- **Integrated Development Environment (IDE)**: SageMaker provides a web-based IDE (Jupyter notebooks) for building and testing models interactively.

- **Training and Tuning**: SageMaker provides built-in algorithms, pre-built models, and the ability to train models using your own data. It also includes automatic hyperparameter tuning to find the best model configurations.

- **Model Deployment**: SageMaker simplifies model deployment by automatically provisioning and scaling hosting environments. It allows for easy A/B testing, multi-model deployment, and real-time inference.

- **SageMaker Studio**: A comprehensive visual interface for managing all aspects of machine learning workflows, from data labeling to model monitoring.

2. Amazon Rekognition: Image and Video Analysis Amazon Rekognition is a service that enables developers to easily add image and video analysis capabilities to their applications. It uses deep learning models to analyze visual data and identify objects, people, scenes, and activities in images and videos.

Key Features of Amazon Rekognition:

- **Facial Recognition**: Detect and compare faces in images and videos to enable use cases such as user authentication, security, and customer insights.

- **Labeling and Object Detection**: Identify thousands of objects, scenes, and activities in images and videos (e.g., "dog", "car", "beach").

- **Text in Images**: Detect and extract text in images (e.g., signs, documents) using optical character recognition (OCR).

- **Real-Time Video Analysis**: Analyze video streams in real-time to identify objects, faces, and activities, ideal for surveillance and monitoring systems.

3. Amazon Polly: Text-to-Speech Amazon Polly is a service that turns text into lifelike speech using deep learning models. It supports multiple languages and voice types, making it suitable for building voice-enabled applications, interactive voice responses, and audio for media content.

Key Features of Amazon Polly:

- **Natural Sounding Voices**: Polly provides high-quality, natural-sounding voices that are customizable to suit various applications.

- **Multiple Languages and Accents**: Polly supports over 30 languages and a wide range of accents and dialects.
- **Real-Time Streaming**: Polly can stream speech in real-time, making it suitable for voice-enabled applications and services.
- **Neural Text-to-Speech**: Polly uses neural network-based deep learning models to provide more realistic and expressive speech synthesis.

4. Amazon Lex: Conversational Interfaces Amazon Lex is a service for building conversational interfaces into applications using voice and text. Lex is the same technology that powers **Amazon Alexa** and enables developers to create chatbots and virtual assistants.

Key Features of Amazon Lex:

- **Speech and Text Recognition**: Lex can recognize text and speech, allowing you to build interactive, multi-turn conversations.
- **Intents and Slots**: Lex uses intents (what the user wants to do) and slots (parameters related to the intent) to create dynamic conversational flows.
- **Integration with AWS Services**: Lex integrates with other AWS services like Lambda, Polly, and DynamoDB, allowing you to add backend functionality to your chatbot or assistant.

- **Automatic Scaling**: Lex automatically scales to handle different levels of conversation volume, from a few requests to thousands per second.

Building ML Models: Training and Deploying Models in the Cloud

Building machine learning models involves several key stages: data collection, data preprocessing, training, evaluation, and deployment. AWS provides the tools and infrastructure to manage each of these stages.

1. Data Collection and Preprocessing Before building a machine learning model, you need to gather and clean data. AWS offers several services for data collection and preprocessing:

- **Amazon S3**: Store large datasets in scalable, low-cost object storage.
- **AWS Glue**: A fully managed ETL (extract, transform, load) service for preparing data.
- **Amazon Redshift**: A fully managed data warehouse for storing and querying large datasets.

2. Model Training with Amazon SageMaker Once your data is ready, you can use **Amazon SageMaker** to train your model. SageMaker supports built-in algorithms for common tasks such as classification, regression, and clustering, as well as support for popular ML frameworks like TensorFlow, PyTorch, and MXNet.

Steps to Train a Model with SageMaker:

1. **Prepare Data**: Load your data from S3 or other sources and preprocess it using SageMaker's data processing tools.

2. **Choose an Algorithm**: Select from SageMaker's built-in algorithms or bring your own custom algorithm.

3. **Train the Model**: Use SageMaker's **managed training** to spin up instances and train your model. SageMaker automatically handles the underlying infrastructure.

4. **Evaluate the Model**: After training, evaluate the model's performance using metrics such as accuracy, precision, and recall.

3. Model Deployment with SageMaker Once your model is trained and evaluated, you can deploy it to an endpoint for real-time inference or batch processing:

- **Real-Time Inference**: Deploy the model to a **SageMaker Endpoint** to make predictions in real-time.
- **Batch Inference**: Use **SageMaker Batch Transform** to make predictions on large datasets in batch mode.

4. Continuous Monitoring and Retraining Machine learning models need to be monitored and retrained periodically to ensure they remain accurate over time. **Amazon CloudWatch** can be used to monitor the performance of your deployed models, and you can use **SageMaker Pipelines** to automate the retraining process.

Real-World Example: Using AWS Rekognition for Facial Recognition in Security Apps

Scenario: A **security company** wants to build a mobile application that uses facial recognition to authenticate users and monitor restricted areas. The company decides to use **Amazon Rekognition** to handle the facial recognition part of the application.

Step 1: Collecting Training Data The company collects images of authorized personnel for facial recognition. They upload these images to **Amazon S3** and use **Rekognition** to create a facial database.

Step 2: Setting Up Rekognition for Facial Analysis Using **Amazon Rekognition**, the company sets up facial analysis functionality. Rekognition can detect faces in images, compare them against stored data, and identify whether the faces match.

- **Face Detection**: Rekognition detects faces in security camera feeds or uploaded images.
- **Face Comparison**: When a new image is uploaded (e.g., a photo taken from the mobile app), Rekognition

compares the image against the database of known faces to authenticate users.

Step 3: Real-Time Monitoring with Rekognition For monitoring restricted areas, the company sets up a real-time video stream using **Amazon Kinesis Video Streams**, and **Rekognition Video** is used to analyze the video stream in real-time to detect faces and match them with authorized personnel.

Step 4: Integrating with Mobile App The company integrates **AWS Amplify** with the mobile app to manage the user interface and interaction with Rekognition. The app uses **Amazon Cognito** for user authentication and integrates Rekognition's facial recognition API to authenticate users and grant access to secure areas.

Step 5: Improving Accuracy and Security To enhance security and reduce false positives, the company configures **multi-factor authentication (MFA)** via **Amazon Cognito**, combining facial recognition with another form of verification (e.g., a PIN code or fingerprint).

Step 6: Monitoring and Logging The company uses **AWS CloudWatch** to monitor the performance of the Rekognition API and logs events such as authentication attempts and access control actions. Alerts are set up to notify the security team of any unauthorized access attempts.

221

Outcome: By leveraging **Amazon Rekognition** for facial recognition, the company improves its security operations, streamlining user authentication and providing a real-time monitoring system that enhances both user convenience and safety.

In this chapter, we've explored **AWS Machine Learning services**, including **Amazon SageMaker** for model building, **Rekognition** for image and video analysis, **Polly** for text-to-speech, and **Lex** for conversational interfaces. We discussed how to build and deploy machine learning models in the cloud and provided a real-world example of using **Rekognition** for facial recognition in security apps. By leveraging AWS's powerful machine learning tools, developers can create AI-driven applications without the need for managing complex infrastructure. In the next chapters, we will dive deeper into additional AI and ML services, including **AWS Deep Learning AMIs** and **Amazon Comprehend** for natural language processing.

CHAPTER 23

AWS FOR BIG DATA AND ANALYTICS

In this chapter, we will explore the powerful **AWS tools** for big data processing and analytics, such as **Amazon Redshift**, **Amazon EMR**, **Amazon Athena**, and **Amazon Kinesis**. These tools help you manage, process, and analyze large datasets efficiently, enabling you to extract valuable insights for your business. We will also discuss how to set up **data lakes** and **data warehouses** using AWS services and structure large datasets for optimal querying. Finally, we will look at a real-world example of analyzing **website traffic** and **customer behavior** using AWS analytics tools.

Introduction to AWS Big Data Tools: Redshift, EMR, Athena, and Kinesis

AWS Big Data Ecosystem AWS provides a variety of services tailored to handle different aspects of big data, including data storage, processing, and analytics. These tools are scalable, cost-efficient, and integrated into the AWS ecosystem, making it easier for organizations to build big data solutions in the cloud.

223

1. Amazon Redshift: Data Warehousing Amazon Redshift is a fully managed data warehouse service that allows you to run complex queries on structured data, store large datasets, and scale as your data grows.

Key Features:

- **Columnar Storage**: Redshift uses columnar storage to compress data, improving performance for analytical queries.
- **Scalable**: You can scale the number of nodes in your Redshift cluster to handle growing data volumes.
- **SQL-Based Queries**: Redshift supports SQL queries, so you can use familiar query languages to analyze large datasets.
- **Integration with BI Tools**: Redshift integrates with popular business intelligence (BI) tools like Tableau and Looker, making it easier to visualize your data.

Use Case: Redshift is ideal for building data warehouses that support complex analytics and reporting, such as analyzing large datasets from e-commerce platforms, customer behavior, and financial data.

2. Amazon EMR: Big Data Processing Amazon Elastic MapReduce (EMR) is a cloud-native big data platform that makes it easy to process vast amounts of data using distributed computing frameworks like **Apache Hadoop**, **Spark**, **Hive**, and **HBase**.

Key Features:

- **Scalable Compute**: EMR clusters can be scaled up or down based on your data processing needs.
- **Managed Frameworks**: EMR supports popular frameworks like Hadoop and Spark for processing and analyzing unstructured data at scale.
- **Data Integration**: EMR integrates seamlessly with data storage services like **Amazon S3** for storing input and output data.
- **Customizable**: You can customize the environment by installing additional libraries and frameworks on your EMR cluster.

Use Case: EMR is perfect for processing and analyzing massive datasets, such as log analysis, ETL (Extract, Transform, Load) tasks, and batch data processing.

3. Amazon Athena: Serverless Querying Amazon Athena is an interactive query service that allows you to analyze large amounts of **S3**-stored data using **SQL**. Athena is serverless, meaning you don't have to manage any infrastructure or compute resources.

Key Features:

- **SQL-Based Queries**: Athena supports standard SQL syntax, so you can quickly query data stored in **S3** without needing to move or transform the data.

- **Serverless**: No need to provision or manage servers. Athena automatically scales based on the query load.

- **Pay-per-Query**: Athena charges based on the amount of data scanned, making it cost-effective for ad-hoc queries or small-to-medium datasets.

- **Integration with Glue**: Athena integrates with **AWS Glue** for cataloging data, making it easier to manage and query structured, semi-structured, and unstructured data.

Use Case: Athena is best suited for ad-hoc querying of data stored in **S3**, such as analyzing event logs, accessing historical sales data, or running exploratory analytics.

4. Amazon Kinesis: Real-Time Data Streaming Amazon Kinesis is a set of services designed for real-time data streaming, enabling you to collect, process, and analyze streaming data with low latency.

Key Features:

- **Kinesis Data Streams**: Allows you to capture and process real-time data streams (e.g., website activity, sensor data) and store them for further processing.

- **Kinesis Data Firehose**: A fully managed service that loads streaming data into **S3**, **Redshift**, **Elasticsearch**, or other destinations.

- **Kinesis Data Analytics**: Enables real-time analytics on streaming data using SQL-like queries.

Use Case: Kinesis is ideal for real-time analytics use cases, such as monitoring website traffic in real-time, analyzing sensor data, or tracking user activity on mobile apps.

Setting Up Data Lakes and Warehouses: Structuring and Querying Large Datasets

1. Data Lakes with Amazon S3 A **data lake** is a centralized repository that allows you to store all your structured, semi-structured, and unstructured data at scale. AWS S3 is commonly used to build data lakes because of its durability, scalability, and cost-effectiveness.

Steps to Set Up a Data Lake in AWS:

1. **Create an S3 Bucket**: Start by creating an S3 bucket to store your data.
2. **Organize Data**: Structure the data in your S3 bucket by creating folders for different types of data (e.g., raw data, processed data, logs).

3. **Catalog Data with AWS Glue**: Use **AWS Glue** to catalog your data and create metadata for easy querying with tools like Athena or Redshift.

4. **Integrate with Analytics Tools**: Connect your data lake to services like Athena, Redshift, or EMR to perform advanced analytics and processing.

2. Data Warehouses with Amazon Redshift A data warehouse is a centralized repository for structured data, optimized for querying and reporting. **Amazon Redshift** is one of the most widely used data warehousing services on AWS, designed for running complex analytical queries on large datasets.

Steps to Set Up a Data Warehouse in AWS:

1. **Create a Redshift Cluster**: Launch an Amazon Redshift cluster through the AWS Management Console.

2. **Load Data**: Load data into Redshift from sources like S3, DynamoDB, or via **Amazon Kinesis** for real-time data streaming.

3. **Create Tables and Schemas**: Organize your data into tables and schemas, optimized for fast querying.

4. **Perform Queries**: Use SQL to perform complex queries, aggregations, and joins on large datasets stored in your Redshift data warehouse.

Real-World Example: Analyzing Website Traffic and Customer Behavior Using AWS Analytics Tools

Let's consider a **marketing company** that wants to analyze website traffic and customer behavior to gain insights into user engagement and improve marketing strategies.

Step 1: Collect Website Traffic Data

- The company uses **Amazon Kinesis Data Streams** to collect real-time data on website traffic, including page views, user clicks, and session duration.
- The data is sent to **Amazon S3** for storage and is organized in folders by date and type of event.

Step 2: Process and Analyze Data in Real-Time

- The company uses **Kinesis Data Analytics** to analyze the streaming data in real time. For example, they may query the number of active users on the site at any given moment or monitor session duration to identify drop-off points.
- Kinesis integrates with **Amazon Redshift** for storing processed data, where the marketing team can perform more complex analyses.

Step 3: Set Up a Data Warehouse

- The company sets up **Amazon Redshift** as a data warehouse to store and analyze historical customer behavior data. They load data from **S3** into Redshift and use SQL queries to calculate key metrics such as conversion rates, time spent on product pages, and the impact of specific marketing campaigns.

- Redshift's powerful SQL engine allows the team to create complex reports and dashboards that provide insights into user behavior across different regions, devices, and traffic sources.

Step 4: Querying with Amazon Athena

- The company uses **Amazon Athena** for ad-hoc querying on data stored in **S3**. For instance, they might want to quickly analyze website traffic trends or identify patterns in customer browsing behavior over the past week.

- Athena's serverless model makes it easy to run SQL queries on S3 data without provisioning or managing servers.

Step 5: Integrating with BI Tools

- The marketing team integrates **Amazon Redshift** with **Tableau**, a popular BI tool, to visualize the results of their queries. This allows them to create interactive dashboards and reports that help inform decision-making.

- The dashboards display key metrics such as traffic sources, conversion rates, and user engagement, helping the team optimize marketing campaigns and improve website design.

Outcome:

- The company can now process and analyze large datasets in real time, gaining insights into customer behavior and website performance. By using **Kinesis, Redshift**, and **Athena**, they can make data-driven decisions to enhance their marketing strategies, improve user engagement, and boost conversions.

In this chapter, we've explored **AWS Big Data tools** such as **Redshift, EMR, Athena**, and **Kinesis**. We also discussed how to set up **data lakes** and **data warehouses** for large datasets and how to query and process that data efficiently. The real-world example showed how AWS analytics tools can be used to analyze website traffic and customer behavior, empowering businesses to optimize their operations and make informed decisions. In the next chapters, we will explore more advanced big data use cases, including machine learning with large datasets and integrating AWS analytics tools with external data sources.

CHAPTER 24

DEPLOYING AND MANAGING MICROSERVICES ON AWS

In this chapter, we will explore the world of **microservices architecture** and how to deploy and manage microservices on AWS using services like **Amazon ECS (Elastic Container Service)** and **Amazon EKS (Elastic Kubernetes Service)**. Microservices architecture is a modern approach to building applications where individual components (or services) are independent, modular, and communicate with each other via APIs. We will also dive into a real-world example of breaking a **monolithic application** into microservices using AWS.

Introduction to Microservices: What Are Microservices and Their Benefits?

What Are Microservices? A **microservices architecture** is an approach to designing and building applications as a collection of small, independent services that can be developed, deployed, and scaled independently. Each service in a microservices architecture is responsible for a specific function and communicates with other services via APIs.

232

Unlike **monolithic** applications, where all components are tightly coupled and part of a single codebase, microservices are decoupled, meaning each service operates independently and can be maintained and updated separately.

Key Characteristics of Microservices:

1. **Independence**: Each microservice is developed, deployed, and scaled independently. This allows for faster development cycles, better fault isolation, and easier updates.

2. **Decoupling**: Microservices communicate with each other through lightweight protocols (often RESTful APIs or message queues), making it easier to manage and scale them.

3. **Technology Agnostic**: Different microservices can be developed using different programming languages or technologies that best suit the specific service's requirements.

4. **Scalability**: Microservices can be scaled individually based on demand, allowing for more efficient resource utilization.

Benefits of Microservices:

- **Faster Development and Deployment**: Independent services can be developed and deployed concurrently,

233

reducing the time it takes to release new features or fix issues.

- **Flexibility in Technology Choices**: Teams can use different technologies for each microservice, depending on their specific needs (e.g., one service might use Python while another uses Node.js).

- **Better Fault Isolation**: Since microservices are isolated, a failure in one service doesn't affect others. This improves system resilience.

- **Improved Scalability**: Microservices can be scaled independently, allowing for more efficient resource usage based on specific service demand.

- **Easier Maintenance and Updates**: Since each microservice is small and focused, it's easier to understand, maintain, and update the code.

Using ECS and EKS: Deploying Containerized Microservices with ECS (Elastic Container Service) and EKS (Elastic Kubernetes Service)

When it comes to deploying and managing microservices, containers have become the standard way to package and deploy applications. AWS offers **Amazon ECS** and **Amazon EKS** to manage and orchestrate containers, making it easier to deploy microservices at scale.

1. Amazon ECS (Elastic Container Service): **ECS** is a fully managed container orchestration service that supports Docker containers. It makes it easy to run, scale, and manage containerized applications on AWS. ECS abstracts away the complexity of managing containers, making it simpler to deploy and manage microservices.

Key Features of Amazon ECS:

- **Managed Cluster Management**: ECS manages the clusters of EC2 instances or Fargate instances that run your containers, handling the scheduling and deployment of services.
- **Service Discovery**: ECS provides service discovery capabilities to allow services within your architecture to locate and communicate with each other.
- **Auto Scaling**: ECS can automatically scale the number of containers running based on CPU and memory utilization, ensuring your application remains performant even under heavy load.
- **Integrated with AWS Services**: ECS integrates seamlessly with other AWS services, such as **AWS IAM** for access control, **CloudWatch** for monitoring, and **AWS Fargate** for serverless containers.

How to Deploy Microservices Using ECS:

1. **Create ECS Cluster**: In the ECS console, create an ECS cluster to manage your container instances or configure AWS Fargate for serverless compute.

2. **Create Docker Images**: Build Docker images for each microservice in your application.

3. **Push Images to Amazon ECR**: Use **Amazon Elastic Container Registry (ECR)** to store your Docker images.

4. **Define ECS Task Definitions**: A task definition is a blueprint for your application, describing which Docker image to use, the amount of resources (CPU, memory) needed, and any environment variables.

5. **Create ECS Services**: Define ECS services that will run your containers. ECS will handle the scheduling, scaling, and updating of your microservices.

2. Amazon EKS (Elastic Kubernetes Service): **Amazon EKS** is a fully managed Kubernetes service that enables you to run and scale containerized applications using Kubernetes, an open-source container orchestration platform. EKS provides the power of Kubernetes with the ease of AWS's managed infrastructure.

Key Features of Amazon EKS:

- **Fully Managed Kubernetes**: EKS manages the Kubernetes control plane, allowing you to focus on deploying and managing microservices.

236

- **Scalability**: EKS scales automatically based on demand, allowing for efficient resource management.

- **Ecosystem Integration**: EKS integrates with other AWS services such as **CloudWatch**, **IAM**, and **Fargate**.

- **Multi-AZ Deployment**: EKS ensures that your Kubernetes control plane is highly available across multiple Availability Zones (AZs), providing resilience.

How to Deploy Microservices Using EKS:

1. **Create an EKS Cluster**: Use the AWS Management Console or CLI to create an EKS cluster. This will set up the Kubernetes control plane and worker nodes.

2. **Configure kubectl**: Set up **kubectl** (the Kubernetes command-line tool) to communicate with your EKS cluster.

3. **Deploy Microservices as Pods**: In Kubernetes, microservices are deployed as **pods**. You will define deployment YAML files for each microservice that specify how to run and scale the pod.

4. **Service Discovery**: Kubernetes offers built-in service discovery to allow your microservices to find and communicate with each other.

5. **Autoscaling**: Kubernetes supports **Horizontal Pod Autoscaling** (HPA), automatically scaling the number of pods based on CPU or memory utilization.

Real-World Example: Breaking a Monolithic App into Microservices on AWS

Let's consider a **retail company** that has a **monolithic web application** responsible for handling all operations, including user authentication, order management, and product catalog management. As the company grows, they decide to break the monolithic app into microservices to improve scalability, maintainability, and development speed.

Step 1: Decompose the Monolith into Microservices The retail company breaks the monolithic app into the following microservices:

- **User Service**: Handles user registration, authentication, and profile management.
- **Product Service**: Manages product catalogs, including product details, pricing, and availability.
- **Order Service**: Processes customer orders, payments, and shipment tracking.

Step 2: Containerize the Microservices Each microservice is packaged into a **Docker container**, ensuring that each service is independent and can be developed, tested, and deployed separately.

Step 3: Deploy to ECS The company decides to use **Amazon ECS** to manage the containerized microservices. They:

- Create an ECS cluster to host the containers.
- Push the Docker images for each service to **Amazon ECR** (Elastic Container Registry).
- Define ECS task definitions for each microservice and deploy them as ECS services.

Step 4: Set Up Service Communication The microservices need to communicate with each other. The company configures **AWS CloudMap** for service discovery, allowing services to locate each other using DNS names.

Step 5: Monitor and Scale with ECS The company sets up **CloudWatch** monitoring for each ECS service to track resource utilization and performance. They enable **auto-scaling** based on CPU usage, ensuring that the services can scale up or down depending on traffic and load.

Step 6: Implement CI/CD The company implements **AWS CodePipeline** and **AWS CodeBuild** to automate the deployment process for each microservice, allowing for continuous integration and delivery (CI/CD) of updates and new features.

Step 7: Manage Security and Permissions The company uses **AWS IAM** roles and policies to manage permissions for each microservice, ensuring that only authorized services can access sensitive resources (e.g., S3 buckets, DynamoDB).

Step 8: Deploy and Scale The microservices are deployed on ECS, and the company can scale each service independently based on traffic and load, reducing the chances of bottlenecks or over-provisioning.

Outcome:

- The company now has a **microservices-based architecture** that is more scalable, flexible, and maintainable than the monolithic application.
- With **ECS** and **Fargate**, the company can deploy and manage the microservices without worrying about server management, and they can automatically scale based on demand.

In this chapter, we've explored **microservices architecture** and how AWS services like **Amazon ECS** and **Amazon EKS** can be used to deploy and manage containerized microservices. We also discussed the process of breaking a **monolithic application** into microservices on AWS, using tools like **ECS, ECR,** and **CloudWatch** for monitoring and scaling. Microservices provide flexibility, scalability, and efficiency, making them a powerful approach for modern application development. In the next chapters, we will dive deeper into advanced topics such as **serverless microservices, service meshes**, and **observability** in microservices architectures.

CHAPTER 25

DEVOPS ON AWS - CI/CD PIPELINES

In this chapter, we will explore **DevOps practices** and how they are implemented on AWS using **CI/CD (Continuous Integration and Continuous Delivery)** pipelines. DevOps is a cultural and technical approach to automating the processes of software development and IT operations, aiming to shorten development cycles, improve collaboration between development and operations teams, and ensure higher-quality software releases. On AWS, DevOps practices are facilitated by a set of fully managed services that automate the entire process from code commit to deployment. We will also cover how to set up **CI/CD pipelines** with **AWS CodePipeline** and look at a real-world example of automating the deployment of a web application.

Introduction to DevOps: What is DevOps and Its Importance in AWS?

What is DevOps? DevOps is a combination of **development** (Dev) and **operations** (Ops) practices that emphasizes collaboration, automation, and integration between software

242

developers and IT operations. The goal of DevOps is to shorten the development lifecycle and deliver high-quality software consistently.

Key principles of DevOps:

1. **Collaboration**: Developers, testers, and operations teams work closely together, breaking down silos and improving communication across the entire software delivery pipeline.

2. **Automation**: Automating manual tasks such as code compilation, testing, and deployment ensures that changes can be delivered rapidly and consistently.

3. **Continuous Integration (CI)**: Continuous integration involves regularly integrating code into a shared repository and automatically running tests to detect bugs early in the development process.

4. **Continuous Delivery (CD)**: Continuous delivery ensures that the latest version of the application is always ready for deployment to production, providing quick and reliable delivery cycles.

5. **Monitoring and Feedback**: Monitoring the application in production and gathering feedback is crucial to understanding the performance and quickly responding to issues.

Why is DevOps Important in AWS?

- **Faster Software Delivery**: DevOps practices enable teams to deliver software more quickly and reliably by automating repetitive tasks, such as builds, tests, and deployments.

- **Scalability and Flexibility**: AWS provides a scalable cloud infrastructure that integrates seamlessly with DevOps tools. You can automatically scale your application based on demand and automate infrastructure provisioning and management.

- **High Availability**: With AWS, DevOps teams can deploy applications in multiple regions and Availability Zones (AZs), ensuring high availability and minimizing downtime.

- **Cost Optimization**: By automating the software delivery pipeline, DevOps can reduce operational costs and increase resource utilization, helping businesses to optimize their AWS spending.

Setting Up CI/CD with AWS CodePipeline: Automating Code Builds, Testing, and Deployment

What is AWS CodePipeline? AWS CodePipeline is a fully managed service that automates the software release process by providing a CI/CD pipeline. CodePipeline allows you to model, visualize,. and automate the steps required to release your software, from code commits to production deployment.

Key Features of AWS CodePipeline:

1. **Automated Workflow**: CodePipeline automates the flow of changes from source code to production. It integrates with other AWS services such as **CodeCommit, CodeBuild**, and **Elastic Beanstalk**.

2. **Version Control Integration**: CodePipeline integrates with version control systems such as **AWS CodeCommit, GitHub**, and **Bitbucket**, so that every code change triggers the pipeline.

3. **Parallel Execution**: You can set up stages that run in parallel, making the deployment process faster and more efficient.

4. **Custom Actions**: CodePipeline allows you to create custom actions at any stage of the pipeline, enabling integration with third-party tools or specialized deployment processes.

5. **Approval Workflow**: You can add manual approval steps in the pipeline, ensuring that code changes are reviewed before deployment to production.

Setting Up a Simple CI/CD Pipeline in AWS CodePipeline:

1. **Create a Source Repository**:
   o Use **AWS CodeCommit** to create a Git-based source repository to store your code. You can also use **GitHub** or another version control provider.

2. **Create a Build Project**:

   o Use **AWS CodeBuild** to define a build project. CodeBuild will automatically compile your code, run unit tests, and produce deployable artifacts (such as Docker images or JAR files).

   o Example: Set up a buildspec.yml file to define the build commands and test scripts.

3. **Define the Pipeline Stages**:

   o Create the pipeline in **AWS CodePipeline**, defining stages such as **Source**, **Build**, **Test**, and **Deploy**.

     ▪ **Source Stage**: Define where CodePipeline will pull the source code from (e.g., CodeCommit repository or GitHub).

     ▪ **Build Stage**: Connect CodeBuild to compile the code and run tests.

     ▪ **Deploy Stage**: Set up deployment actions to deploy the build to AWS services like **Elastic Beanstalk**, **ECS**, or **Lambda**.

4. **Automate Deployment**:

   o Set up **Elastic Beanstalk** or **Amazon ECS** as the deployment target. Whenever the build is successful, the deployment stage will automatically push the code to the production environment.

- o You can also configure **manual approval** steps to require human intervention before deploying to production.

5. **Monitoring and Notifications**:

- o Set up **AWS CloudWatch** monitoring to track the performance of the pipeline and deploy process. Additionally, configure **SNS (Simple Notification Service)** to notify your team about the status of the pipeline (success, failure, etc.).

Example CodePipeline Workflow:

1. **Source**: Code is committed to a Git repository (e.g., AWS CodeCommit).

2. **Build**: AWS CodeBuild compiles the code, runs tests, and produces artifacts (e.g., Docker image).

3. **Test**: Unit tests and integration tests are run in parallel to verify the build.

4. **Deploy**: The build artifacts are deployed to the production environment (e.g., EC2, Elastic Beanstalk).

Real-World Example: Automating the Deployment of a Web Application with AWS DevOps Tools

Scenario: A **startup company** has developed a simple web application hosted on **EC2** and wants to automate their deployment process to make it more efficient, reliable, and scalable.

Step 1: Source Control and CodePipeline Setup

- The team stores their source code in **AWS CodeCommit**, a Git-based repository, and uses **AWS CodePipeline** to automate the deployment pipeline.
- Whenever a developer pushes new code to the repository, **CodePipeline** is triggered, starting the build process.

Step 2: Build Automation with CodeBuild

- **AWS CodeBuild** automatically compiles the code, runs unit tests, and generates the application artifact (e.g., a **Docker image**).
- The buildspec.yml file in the repository defines the build commands, such as installing dependencies and running tests.

Step 3: Automated Testing

- In the **test stage**, CodePipeline uses **AWS CodeBuild** to run integration tests, ensuring the application works as expected before it is deployed.
- Automated tests include checking the connectivity to the database, verifying API endpoints, and testing the UI using **Selenium** or other testing frameworks.

Step 4: Deployment to EC2

- The **deploy stage** in CodePipeline automatically deploys the build artifacts to an EC2 instance using **AWS CodeDeploy** or **Elastic Beanstalk**.
- The deployment step ensures that the new version of the application is automatically rolled out, with zero downtime and rollback capabilities if necessary.

Step 5: Monitoring and Notification

- After each deployment, **AWS CloudWatch** monitors the health and performance of the EC2 instance running the web app.
- The team receives notifications through **SNS** if the deployment fails or if there are performance issues in the production environment.

Outcome:

- The company now has an automated, end-to-end **CI/CD pipeline** that reduces the time it takes to deploy code, ensures consistency and reliability in the deployment process, and allows for rapid iteration and improvements to the web app.

- Code changes are automatically tested, built, and deployed without manual intervention, improving development efficiency and minimizing the risk of human error.

In this chapter, we've covered **DevOps** principles and the importance of **CI/CD pipelines** in AWS. We've explored **AWS CodePipeline** and its integration with **CodeBuild, CodeDeploy,** and **Elastic Beanstalk** to automate the entire software delivery pipeline. The real-world example showed how a web application's deployment process can be automated with AWS DevOps tools, reducing manual effort, improving reliability, and enabling faster development cycles. In the next chapters, we will dive deeper into advanced DevOps topics, including **infrastructure as code** with **AWS CloudFormation, monitoring and logging,** and best practices for continuous delivery.

CHAPTER 26

ADVANCED AWS NETWORKING AND SECURITY

In this chapter, we will explore advanced AWS networking and security concepts that are crucial for managing complex infrastructure and protecting mission-critical applications. We will cover key topics such as **VPC Peering** and **Transit Gateways** for managing sophisticated networking architectures, **advanced IAM features** for securing user access, and best practices for securing production systems. Finally, we will discuss a real-world example of implementing a **multi-region, highly available application infrastructure** on AWS.

VPC Peering and Transit Gateways: Managing Complex Networking Scenarios

What is a VPC? A **Virtual Private Cloud (VPC)** is a logically isolated network within the AWS cloud where you can launch AWS resources, such as EC2 instances, RDS databases, and Lambda functions. VPCs allow you to control your IP address range, subnets, routing tables, and security settings.

1. VPC Peering: VPC Peering allows you to connect two VPCs within the same AWS region or across different regions. This enables communication between resources in the peered VPCs using private IP addresses, as if they are part of the same network.

Key Features of VPC Peering:

- **Private Communication**: Once VPCs are peered, they can communicate using private IP addresses, eliminating the need for public internet access.
- **Cross-Region Peering**: You can set up VPC peering between VPCs in different AWS regions, allowing for global infrastructure connectivity.
- **No Transitive Peering**: VPC peering does not support transitive routing. If VPC A is peered with VPC B, and VPC B is peered with VPC C, VPC A cannot communicate directly with VPC C through VPC B.

Setting Up VPC Peering:

1. **Create VPCs**: Ensure that both VPCs you want to peer are set up and that they have non-overlapping CIDR blocks.
2. **Initiate Peering Connection**: From the AWS Management Console, navigate to the VPC dashboard, select "Peering Connections," and initiate a new connection between the two VPCs.

3. **Accept Peering Request**: The owner of the other VPC (or you, if you're working within the same AWS account) must accept the peering request.

4. **Update Route Tables**: After establishing the peering connection, update the route tables in both VPCs to allow communication between them.

Use Case: VPC peering is useful for scenarios where multiple AWS accounts or services need to communicate with each other, such as a multi-tenant application or a scenario where one VPC hosts a shared service, like a centralized database, and other VPCs need access.

2. AWS Transit Gateway: The **AWS Transit Gateway** is a central hub for managing complex networking environments, especially when you have multiple VPCs and on-premises networks. Transit Gateway simplifies network management by acting as a hub for connecting VPCs, VPNs, and AWS Direct Connect connections.

Key Features of Transit Gateway:

- **Centralized Management**: It simplifies network routing by centralizing traffic flow between VPCs and on-premises networks.
- **Scalability**: You can scale the Transit Gateway to support many VPCs and thousands of VPN connections.

- **Inter-Region Peering**: Transit Gateway supports cross-region peering, allowing you to connect VPCs in different AWS regions without direct VPC peering.
- **Routing Control**: Transit Gateway provides fine-grained control over routing between VPCs and on-premises networks.

Setting Up Transit Gateway:

1. **Create Transit Gateway**: From the AWS Management Console, create a Transit Gateway in your desired region.
2. **Attach VPCs**: Attach the VPCs you want to connect to the Transit Gateway.
3. **Configure Routing**: Update the route tables in each VPC to send traffic through the Transit Gateway.
4. **Enable Inter-Region Peering (Optional)**: If you need to connect VPCs across different regions, configure inter-region peering between Transit Gateways.

Use Case: Transit Gateway is ideal for large organizations with multiple VPCs that need a simplified way to manage routing and connectivity between them. It's also useful when integrating on-premises networks with AWS cloud infrastructure.

Advanced IAM Features: Using Roles and Federated Identity

1. IAM Roles: **AWS Identity and Access Management (IAM)** allows you to manage access to AWS resources securely. One of the most important IAM features is **IAM Roles**, which define a set of permissions that can be assumed by AWS resources or users.

Key Use Cases for IAM Roles:

- **Cross-Account Access**: IAM roles allow users or resources from one AWS account to access resources in another account. For example, an EC2 instance in one account might assume a role to access an S3 bucket in another account.
- **Service Roles**: AWS services like Lambda or EC2 can assume roles to access other services on your behalf. For example, a Lambda function may need to access an S3 bucket or write logs to CloudWatch.

Setting Up IAM Roles:

1. **Create a Role**: Navigate to the IAM console, and select "Roles" to create a new role.
2. **Attach Policies**: Attach the appropriate policies to define the permissions granted to the role. You can attach AWS-managed policies or custom policies.

3. **Assign the Role**: Assign the role to an AWS resource, such as an EC2 instance or Lambda function, or allow IAM users to assume the role as needed.

2. Federated Identity and SSO (Single Sign-On): **Federated Identity** allows users from external identity providers (such as Google, Facebook, or corporate LDAP directories) to access AWS resources. This eliminates the need for managing IAM users manually and enables **Single Sign-On (SSO)** across applications.

Key Features:

- **Cognito Federated Identities**: AWS **Cognito** provides a solution for federating user identities and managing authentication in your applications.
- **AWS SSO**: AWS Single Sign-On allows you to centrally manage access to AWS accounts and applications, integrating with Active Directory and third-party identity providers.

Setting Up Federated Identity with Amazon Cognito:

1. **Create a User Pool**: In Cognito, create a **User Pool** to handle authentication.
2. **Set Up Federated Identity Providers**: Link external identity providers (e.g., Google, Facebook, Active Directory) to your Cognito user pool.

3. **Enable SSO**: Use **AWS SSO** for managing access to AWS accounts and resources for users authenticated via federated identity providers.

Use Case: Federated identity is useful for scenarios where users need to log in to AWS applications using credentials from third-party services (e.g., social media logins, corporate SSO) without managing multiple sets of credentials.

Security Best Practices for Production Systems: Securing High-Traffic, Mission-Critical Applications

Securing your AWS infrastructure is crucial, especially for **production systems** that handle high volumes of traffic and sensitive data. Below are some best practices to follow when securing these mission-critical applications:

1. Use Security Groups and NACLs:

- **Security Groups**: Act as virtual firewalls for EC2 instances. Ensure that you use the principle of **least privilege**, allowing only necessary inbound and outbound traffic.
- **Network Access Control Lists (NACLs)**: NACLs provide an additional layer of security at the subnet level.

Use NACLs to restrict access based on IP address ranges and improve your network security posture.

2. Enable Encryption:

- **Encrypt Data at Rest**: Use **AWS KMS** to encrypt sensitive data stored in services like S3, EBS, and RDS. This ensures that data is protected, even if unauthorized access occurs.
- **Encrypt Data in Transit**: Use **SSL/TLS** to encrypt data during transmission between clients, EC2 instances, and AWS services.

3. Implement Multi-Factor Authentication (MFA): Enable **MFA** for all AWS accounts, especially for users with high-level permissions. MFA adds an extra layer of security by requiring users to authenticate using a second factor, such as a code from a mobile device.

4. Regularly Rotate Keys and Secrets: Use **AWS Secrets Manager** to manage and rotate secrets, API keys, and credentials. Regular key rotation ensures that compromised credentials are not a persistent vulnerability.

5. Monitor and Audit with AWS CloudTrail: Use **AWS CloudTrail** to record and log all API calls made to AWS services. CloudTrail helps in tracking access to resources and investigating suspicious activities or potential security incidents.

Real-World Example: Implementing a Multi-Region, Highly Available Application Infrastructure

Scenario: A **global e-commerce platform** needs a **highly available** infrastructure that can handle millions of users, process transactions securely, and ensure minimal downtime in case of failure.

Step 1: Set Up Multi-Region VPCs:

- The platform sets up VPCs in **multiple AWS regions** to ensure that if one region experiences an outage, the other region can handle the traffic.
- They use **AWS Transit Gateway** to enable secure and seamless communication between VPCs in different regions.

Step 2: Configure Auto Scaling and Load Balancing:

- **Amazon ECS** is used to deploy the platform's microservices. **Elastic Load Balancers (ELB)** are placed in front of the EC2 instances to distribute traffic evenly across multiple availability zones and regions.
- **Auto Scaling** is configured to automatically scale the number of EC2 instances based on incoming traffic and resource utilization.

Step 3: Secure User Data with Cognito:

- The platform uses **Amazon Cognito** for user authentication, allowing users to log in using social accounts (e.g., Facebook, Google) and ensuring secure access to user accounts and orders.

Step 4: Set Up Cross-Region Replication for Data:

- **Amazon RDS** is deployed with **cross-region replication** to ensure that databases are available in both regions.
- **Amazon S3** is used for storage with **cross-region replication** to ensure data availability and consistency across regions.

Step 5: Implement Monitoring and Disaster Recovery:

- **AWS CloudWatch** monitors application performance, and **AWS CloudTrail** logs API activity for auditing purposes.
- **AWS Backup** is used to automate regular backups of EC2 instances, databases, and application data.
- The platform implements a **disaster recovery plan** with **AWS Route 53** to manage DNS routing between regions in case of failure.

Outcome:

- The e-commerce platform is now highly available and resilient to regional failures. Traffic is automatically routed to healthy regions, user data is encrypted and secure, and the system can scale to meet high demand during peak seasons.

In this chapter, we have explored **advanced networking and security concepts** in AWS, including **VPC Peering, Transit Gateways, IAM roles**, and **federated identity**. We also discussed **security best practices** for securing mission-critical applications and outlined a **real-world example** of building a highly available, multi-region application infrastructure on AWS. These advanced networking and security strategies are key to building robust, scalable, and secure systems on AWS. In the next chapters, we will dive deeper into **advanced IAM configurations, network security**, and **incident response strategies** to further enhance your AWS infrastructure security.

CHAPTER 27

PREPARING FOR THE AWS CERTIFICATION EXAM

In this chapter, we will provide an overview of the **AWS Certification** program, covering the various certifications available for different AWS roles. We will also share effective **study tips and resources** to help you prepare for your AWS exam and improve your chances of success. Finally, we will walk through a **real-world case study** of someone preparing for and passing the **AWS Solutions Architect exam**.

Overview of AWS Certifications: Cloud Practitioner, Solutions Architect, Developer, SysOps

What is AWS Certification? AWS offers certifications that validate your skills and expertise in using AWS cloud services. These certifications are recognized by the industry and help professionals prove their knowledge in various cloud-related roles, ranging from beginner to advanced levels. AWS certifications are highly valuable for anyone looking to advance their career in cloud computing and AWS services.

Available AWS Certifications: AWS offers certifications across four main categories, each focused on specific roles and skill sets:

1. **AWS Certified Cloud Practitioner**:
   o **Level**: Foundational
   o **Target Audience**: Beginners or anyone new to cloud computing.
   o **Focus**: This certification is designed for individuals who want to build a basic understanding of AWS Cloud and its core services. It covers the fundamentals of AWS, cloud architecture, pricing, and security.
   o **Exam Format**: Multiple-choice questions.
   o **Recommended Experience**: None required, although a basic understanding of cloud computing concepts is helpful.

2. **AWS Certified Solutions Architect – Associate**:
   o **Level**: Associate
   o **Target Audience**: Individuals who want to specialize in designing and deploying scalable and cost-efficient systems on AWS.
   o **Focus**: This certification validates your ability to design distributed systems on AWS, manage AWS services, and implement best practices for cloud architecture.
   o **Exam Format**: Multiple-choice and multiple-response questions.

263

o **Recommended Experience**: At least one year of hands-on experience with AWS services.

3. **AWS Certified Developer – Associate**:

o **Level**: Associate

o **Target Audience**: Developers who want to demonstrate their skills in developing cloud-based applications on AWS.

o **Focus**: This certification focuses on writing code for AWS services, managing and deploying applications, and using AWS SDKs for application development.

o **Exam Format**: Multiple-choice and multiple-response questions.

o **Recommended Experience**: At least one year of hands-on experience with AWS services and application development.

4. **AWS Certified SysOps Administrator – Associate**:

o **Level**: Associate

o **Target Audience**: System administrators who want to validate their ability to manage and operate scalable and highly available systems on AWS.

o **Focus**: This certification covers the deployment, management, and operational aspects of AWS environments, including monitoring, automation, and troubleshooting.

- **Exam Format**: Multiple-choice and multiple-response questions.
- **Recommended Experience**: At least one year of hands-on experience in a system administrator role managing AWS resources.

Advanced Certifications: AWS also offers advanced-level certifications for more specialized roles:

- **AWS Certified Solutions Architect – Professional**: Focuses on advanced design concepts and best practices for highly complex AWS systems.
- **AWS Certified DevOps Engineer – Professional**: Focuses on automating processes and improving CI/CD in cloud environments.
- **AWS Certified Advanced Networking – Specialty**: For professionals who focus on complex networking solutions on AWS.
- **AWS Certified Security – Specialty**: For individuals with a deep focus on AWS security.
- **AWS Certified Machine Learning – Specialty**: For those focusing on machine learning and AI with AWS.

Study Tips and Resources: How to Prepare for the AWS Exam

1. Understand the Exam Blueprint: Each AWS certification exam has a detailed blueprint that outlines the topics covered. Start by reviewing the exam guide and blueprint for the certification you are pursuing. AWS provides these blueprints for each exam, and they will help you focus on the key areas.

Key Resources:

- AWS Exam Guides: Available on the AWS certification website.
- Exam Blueprints: Detailed breakdown of the topics covered in the exam.

2. Take Advantage of AWS Training and Free Resources: AWS offers a range of **free and paid training resources** to help you prepare:

- **AWS Training and Certification**: AWS offers online courses and learning paths for each certification. You can also take live, instructor-led courses for a more in-depth learning experience.
- **AWS Whitepapers**: AWS provides technical whitepapers that cover best practices and architectural patterns. Reading these can deepen your understanding of AWS services and their use cases.

266

o   Notable whitepapers: **AWS Well-Architected Framework, AWS Security Best Practices, Architecting for the Cloud.**

3. Use Practice Exams: Taking practice exams will help you get familiar with the exam format and question types. It will also help identify areas where you need to improve your knowledge. AWS offers **official practice exams** that simulate the real exam environment.

- **AWS Practice Exams**: Available through AWS training or third-party platforms.
- **Free Practice Questions**: Many websites and forums (e.g., AWS subreddit, ACloudGuru) offer free practice questions.

4. Hands-On Experience: AWS exams test your practical knowledge, so it's crucial to have hands-on experience with the services covered in the exam. Create a free AWS account to experiment with different AWS services and work on real-world projects.

5. Join Study Groups and Forums: Join online communities and forums where others are studying for AWS certifications. Sharing knowledge, discussing difficult topics, and getting advice from others can significantly enhance your understanding.

- **AWS Certification Discussion Forums**: AWS certification community forums.

- **Study Groups**: Join groups on LinkedIn, Reddit, or platforms like **ACloudGuru** or **Whizlabs** for group study sessions.

6. Set a Study Schedule: Consistency is key when preparing for the AWS certification exams. Set aside time each day or week for study sessions. Break down your study materials into manageable chunks and gradually build your knowledge over time.

Real-World Example: Case Study of Someone Preparing and Passing the AWS Solutions Architect Exam

Background:

John, a DevOps engineer with 2 years of experience in AWS, decided to pursue the **AWS Certified Solutions Architect – Associate** exam to enhance his career prospects. He wanted to improve his cloud architecture skills and gain deeper expertise in designing highly available, cost-effective systems on AWS.

Step 1: Review the Exam Blueprint
John started by reviewing the official exam guide for the **Solutions Architect – Associate** certification. He familiarized himself with the key areas covered in the exam, such as designing high-availability architectures, cost optimization, security, and

deployment strategies. The blueprint helped John understand the major topics, including VPC design, EC2, S3, IAM, and AWS cost management.

Step 2: Study Resources

- **AWS Training**: John enrolled in the AWS Solutions Architect – Associate training course offered by AWS. The course was structured and included video lessons, hands-on labs, and quizzes.
- **AWS Whitepapers**: He read essential AWS whitepapers, including the **Well-Architected Framework**, which helped him understand best practices in cloud architecture.

Step 3: Practice Exams and Hands-On Work

- **AWS Practice Exam**: John took the official AWS practice exam to get a sense of the question format and time management. This helped him gauge his readiness and identify weak areas.
- **Hands-On Labs**: John worked on multiple hands-on labs, deploying EC2 instances, configuring S3 buckets, setting up VPCs, and experimenting with IAM policies. He also used the **AWS Free Tier** to practice without incurring significant costs.

Step   4:   Join   Study   Groups

John joined an online study group where he could discuss questions and scenarios with others. This helped him clarify complex concepts like **AWS Elastic Load Balancing (ELB)**, **Auto Scaling**, and **Route 53**. He also participated in mock exams and group discussions to reinforce his learning.

Step   5:   Exam   Day

On exam day, John felt confident due to his structured preparation. He made sure to review the exam guide one last time and used the practice exams to manage his time during the test. The exam consisted of multiple-choice questions that tested his knowledge of real-world AWS use cases, architectural best practices, and problem-solving skills.

Result:

John passed the **AWS Certified Solutions Architect – Associate** exam with flying colors. His preparation strategy, which included studying AWS resources, hands-on labs, and practice exams, helped him gain the necessary skills and confidence to succeed.

In this chapter, we've covered the **AWS Certification program**, including the different certification levels such as **Cloud Practitioner, Solutions Architect, Developer**, and **SysOps**. We also shared effective **study tips and resources** to help you prepare for the AWS exam, from understanding the exam blueprint to leveraging practice exams and AWS training. The real-world case study of **John preparing for and passing the AWS Solutions Architect exam** showed how structured preparation can lead to success. In the next chapters, we will explore advanced certification topics and how to further enhance your skills post-certification.